Nassau W. Senior, Alexis de Tocqueville

Correspondence and Conversations of Alexis de Tocqueville

with Nassau William Senior from 1834 to 1859. Vol. 1

Nassau W. Senior, Alexis de Tocqueville

Correspondence and Conversations of Alexis de Tocqueville
with Nassau William Senior from 1834 to 1859. Vol. 1

ISBN/EAN: 9783337219376

Printed in Europe, USA, Canada, Australia, Japan

Cover: Foto ©ninafisch / pixelio.de

More available books at **www.hansebooks.com**

CORRESPONDENCE & CONVERSATIONS OF

ALEXIS DE TOCQUEVILLE

WITH

NASSAU WILLIAM SENIOR

FROM 1834 TO 1859

EDITED BY

M. C. M. SIMPSON

IN TWO VOLUMES—VOLUME I.

LONDON
HENRY S. KING & CO., 65 CORNHILL
1872

LONDON: PRINTED BY
SPOTTISWOODE AND CO., NEW-STREET SQUARE
AND PARLIAMENT STREET

PREFACE.

ONE DAY in the year 1833 a knock was heard at the door of the Chambers in which Mr. Senior was sitting at work, and a young man entered who announced himself in these terms: 'Je suis Alexis de Tocqueville, et je viens faire votre connaissance.' He had no other introduction.

Alexis de Tocqueville was at that time unknown to fame. His great work on America had not yet appeared.

Mr. Senior, however, perceived at once the extraordinary qualities of his new acquaintance. M. de Tocqueville became a frequent visitor in Mr. Senior's house, and the intimacy thus begun was continued by letter or conversation without interruption (indeed every year drew it closer) until the premature death of Tocqueville in 1859.

Soon after that event Mr. Senior collected and arranged his letters and conversations with a view to their publication at some future time: some extracts from them appeared in the 'Memoir of Tocqueville' published in 1861.

I have thought it would add to the interest of the correspondence to print Mr. Senior's letters, which were sent to me by M. de Beaumont after my father's death. I wish that I could have reproduced the French as well as the English originals, as I cannot hope in a translation to give an idea of the force or the grace of M. de Tocqueville's style.

Mrs. Grote has kindly permitted me to insert in these volumes her notes of conversations in 1849 and 1854.

I have included Mr. Senior's journal of a visit which we paid to Madame de Tocqueville after the death of the great philosopher. She had collected round her three or four of his most intimate friends, and he seemed to be still amongst us, for we talked of him continually and he was never absent from our thoughts. How much we wished that we could once more hear his voice, which, sweet, low, and varied in its tones, added so much to the charm of his conversation.

In person he was small and delicate. He had very thick and rather long black hair, soft yet brilliant dark eyes, and a finely marked brow. The upper lip was long and the mouth wide, but sensitive and expressive. His manner was full of kindness and playfulness, and his fellow-countrymen used to say of him that he was a perfect specimen of the 'gentilhomme de l'ancien régime.'

Although he had a keen sense of humour, his countenance was sad in repose. Indeed the 'fond' of his character was sad, partly from sensitiveness, partly from ill-health. The period in which his lot was cast was not calculated to raise his spirits; he foresaw, only too clearly, the troubled future in store for France.

The convulsions of the last two years, while they would have deeply pained, would not have surprised him; and though France could ill afford to lose such a man, his friends may find some consolation in the reflection that he is at rest.

M. C. M. SIMPSON.

KENSINGTON: *May* 7, 1872.

MR. SENIOR'S INTRODUCTORY NOTE TO THE CONVERSATIONS,

Written in 1859.

I WAS honoured by the friendship of Alexis de Tocqueville for twenty-six years—from 1833 to 1859—but I did not attempt to preserve his conversations until 1848.

In the May of that year I visited Paris, and I was so much struck by the strange things which I saw and heard, that I took notes of them, which swelled into a regular Journal.

The practice once begun, I continued during my subsequent travels, and these volumes contain perhaps the most valuable part of my Journals—that which was contributed to them by M. de Tocqueville.

Of course his conversation loses enormously by translation. Its elegance and finesse could not be retained, but its knowledge and wisdom were less-volatile, and I have reason to hope that they have been, to a certain extent, preserved.

In general I sent M. de Tocqueville my reports as they were written, and he corrected them before they were copied.

In one or two cases he made notes on the fair copy.

That nothing of his might be lost I have reproduced the originals with his notes.

NASSAU WILLIAM SENIOR.

CONTENTS

OF

THE FIRST VOLUME.

Letters from 1834 *to* 1848.

	PAGE
Mr. Senior's criticisms on the 'Démocratie'	3
M. de Tocqueville's answer	6
On M. de Beaumont's 'Marie'	10
On the 'Bien des pauvres'	10
Poor Law Report	12
Timidity of English Ministry	14
Whig Ministry necessarily more honest than Tory	14
Reform Bill in reality a Revolution	15
Prosperity of France	16
Conversion of the Funds	17
Instability of French Ministry	18
Absorption of M. de Tocqueville in preparing the latter volumes of the 'Démocratie'	20
Further criticisms on the 'Démocratie'	22
Comparison of the French and English	22
Indifference of the general public in England to conquest	23
Causes which regulate wages	24
Treaty for the suppression of the Slave Trade	27
Should M. Guizot have resigned?	27
Mr. Senior's opinion that he should not	29
Article on Ireland	30
Anxiety in France	32
Want of Aristocratic element	33
Excess of the Monarchical	34

	PAGE
False notions of the French on Political Economy	35
Causes of Revolution of 1848	35
Speech of M. de Tocqueville, January 27, 1848	36
Government of Louis Philippe	37
Émeute of April 16	39
Attack on the Assembly, May 15	40

Journal in Paris, 1848.

Tocqueville's account of May 15	41
Why the Assembly should work ill	44
Dinner at Tocqueville's	44
Characters of French Statesmen	45
Expectations of a street fight	46
Frenchmen never bold on the defensive	47
Garde Mobile	48
Character of Lamartine	49
Comparison between the Revolutions 1789 and 1848	50
Contempt has taken the place of hatred against the upper classes	51
Decrease in the influence of women	51

Letters in 1849.

Foreign policy of English Ministers	53
Universal listlessness in France	54
Probable character of the new Assembly	55
Increase of the influence of the upper classes	56
English politics	58

Notes by Mrs. Grote.

M. de Tocqueville's account of the days of June	60
Story of the 'Rouge' Concierge	62

Journal in Paris, 1849.

Terms of peace between Austria and Piedmont	66
Prussian aggrandisement dangerous to France	67
Tocqueville's difficulties as a speaker	68
Distinction between noble and roturier	69
Exertion of public speaking	69
Bores in the House	70

Contents of the First Volume.

Letter from Mr. Senior, December 1849.

	PAGE
Bugeaud's account of February 24	71

Journal in Paris, 1850.

Tocqueville disapproves of what is going on	73
Believes that the present Constitution might be made to work	73
Danger of historical parallels	75
Objects of the Conservative party	75
Probable result of an Émeute	76
Greek affairs	77
Absolute government of Louis Philippe	78
Its foundation a quick sand	78
Popularity of Lord Normanby	79
All parties conspiring	81
No end to Revolution in our time	81
No hero cast up by the Revolution of 1848	82
Foreign policy of Lord Palmerston	82
Position of clergy in France	83
Depression of the Duc de Broglie	86
Revolution of 1789 has never ceased	87
Review of French History from 1789 to 1850	87
Greek affairs	91
Preference of égalité to liberty	92
Definition of égalité	93

Journal in Normandy, 1850.

Description of Château de Tocqueville	99
The Reign of Terror	100
New election law	100
Prospects of the four great parties	101
Republicans powerless	101
Orleanists unpopular	101
Legitimists associated with feudalism	102
Probable re-election of the President	103
Probabilities of a Fusion	104
State of Religion	106
Re-action after 1789	106
Religion as an engine of Government	107

	PAGE
Observances of Catholicism	107
Farming at Tocqueville	108
Condition of the peasantry	109
Extent and value of estate	110
Agriculture affected by instability	111
Thiers' History of the Empire	112
Character of Napoleon I.	113
Tocqueville hopes to write his history	114
Country-house life	115
Paucity of modern great men	116
Character of Peel	116
Character of Wellington	117
Of Soult, Bugeaud, and Lamoricière	118
Nicholas intolerant of Constitutional Monarchy	119
French Army	120
Warlike propensities of the French	121
New education law	121
École Polytechnique	122
Exclusiveness of country society	122
French marriages	123
Tocqueville as leader of a party	124
His love of work	125
Cherbourg	127
Valuable against England	128
Revolution of 1848	129
The National Guard revolutionary	130
How the Monarchy might have been saved	131
The Banquet abandoned	132
Fire in the Boulevard des Capucines	132
Unpopularity of Louis Philippe's Government	133
It was a plutocracy	134
Paid representatives	135
Collective voting	135
Tendency of properties to coalesce	136
Danger of mortgages to small proprietors	136
Society formerly much more amusing	137
Influence of women—Madame Récamier	138
A wedding near Limoges	138
French households	139
Scanty population	140
Golden age of French literature	141
Deterioration in the present day	141
French poetry	142

Contents of the First Volume. xiii

	PAGE
Bayeux tapestry	144
Journey to St. Aubin	147
Château of St. Aubin	149
Village schoolmistress	151
Death of Louis Philippe	152
His character and conduct	152
Execution of a conveyance	154
Position of lawyers	157
M. Anisson on Protection	158
His Parliamentary life	158
Qualities valued in Parisian society	160
Farming superior to that of Tocqueville	161
Careers open to gentlemen	163
Château de Caudebec	165
Unprofitableness of forests	166
Country clergy	167
Early life of M. Anisson	167
Oak at Allonville	168
No country visiting	168
Monsieur, Madame, and Mademoiselle	169
Difficulty of recording conversation	179

Letters in 1850.

Normandy journal	171
The Tocquevilles agree to meet Mr. Senior in Italy	171
No-popery agitation	174

Journal at Sorrento, 1851.

Anti-Catholic movement	179
Miserable example of intolerance	180
Superiority of Protestant populations	180
Effects of persecution	181
Mischievous effects of English bigotry	182
Dulness of English sermons	183
Worldliness of English clergymen	184
Protestantism not ascetic	184
Strength of religious feeling in England	185
Protestantism a religion of opposition	185
Celibacy of clergy	186
Letter to Archbishop Whately on the above conversation	187

Contents of the First Volume.

	PAGE
Vote of want of confidence	188
Struggle between the President and the Assembly	189
Louis Napoleon learned to estimate free enterprise in England	189
He is determined to be his own sole Minister	190
Assembly should have made a stand in 1849	190
Two modes in which it might coerce the President	190
A dissolution impracticable	191
Plans of usurpation	192
Unwise expenditure	192
Prophecy of a Coup d'État	193
Its mode described	194
Mistaken ideas of President's character	195
Specimen of Neapolitan middle class	196
Anecdote of a Legitimist	197
Salerno	199
Pæstum	200
Murder of Mr. and Mrs. Hunt	201
Future Constitution of France	203
Aristocracy has suffered the most	203
Poor Law	204
Right to relief	204
Injurious effects of charity	205
Benefits of a Poor Law	205
Death by starvation	206
Asceticism and Confession	207
Uneasiness of Tocqueville at want of news	208
Hopes that the Assembly will win the day	208
President would destroy liberty	209
Tocqueville would support the Constitution	209
Blunders of the Assembly	210
Defects of the Constitution	211
News from Paris	214
Ministers mere clerks	214
Sorrentine boatmen	215
Beggars at Amalfi	217
Story of Ben Ferrhat	218
Interpellations addressed to the Ministry	221
Fears that Representative body will prove still weaker	221
Revision of the Constitution	222
French prose writers	223
Ampère surprised by the Revolution of 1848	224
Resemblance of 1851 to 1795	225
In 1795 the army decided	227

Contents of the First Volume.

	PAGE
Defence of a National Guard	227
President asks for money	227
A decisive struggle at hand	228
Talleyrand	228
Society under the Empire not amusing	229
Tocqueville not responsible for the Roman expedition	231
He had not taken office	232
Austria would have undertaken it	232
The French spared the town	233
Tocqueville pressed reform on the Pope	233
Rights against the Roman Republic	234
Concessions demanded by Tocqueville	235
Obstinacy and superstition of the Pope	236
Unfavourable influence of Naples	238
Attitude of Austria	239
Louis Napoleon yielded everything	239
Tocqueville's intentions had he remained Minister	239
Grandeur of Thebes	241
Excellence of Russian army	241
Religious feeling in Russia	242
Supposititious French Memoirs	242
Louis XVIII. the only Constitutional King of France	243
Distinction of the Orleans family	243

Letters in 1851.

Religious storm in England	244
Tocqueville's return to France	245

Journal in Paris, May 1851.

Commercial state of France	247
Obscurity of political horizon	248
President considers himself re-eligible	248
If re-elected the Constitution will be violated	249
Qualities required for a mixed Government	250
Probable revision of the Constitution	251
Irritating conduct of the Ministers	252
Position of the four Political parties in France	253
Desire for the revision	254
Mischievousness of precedents	255
Three modes in which Louis Napoleon might retain power	256

	PAGE
He will not obtain a majority	257
Advantages of an Upper Chamber	257
Power of a single Chamber to resist encroachment	258
Fusion does not gain ground	258
Law of May 31	259
Inconsistent with universal suffrage	259
Probable that the President will use force	260
The Comte de Paris the best Sovereign	260

Letters in 1851 (continued).

Tocqueville employed on the revision	262
Effect of his Report in England	263
Probable illegal re-election of President	264
President proof against Constitutional ideas	265
No illegal movement should be permitted	266
Two opposite motives for desiring the revision	267
Nations accustomed to revolutions	268
English intolerance	268
Tocqueville's opinions in former conversations	269
Want of aristocracies in Europe	270
Gravity of present situation	273

Correspondence and Conversations

of

A. de Tocqueville.

CORRESPONDENCE.

Alexis de Tocqueville to N. W. Senior.

March 24, 1834.

My dear Mr. Senior,—I hope that you have not yet entirely forgotten one who will always remember your kind reception with gratitude. I take to-day the liberty of asking you to bestow a portion of the same good will on my countryman, M. Guéry.

M. Guéry, who is an advocate practising in the Cour Royale in Paris, is the author of a book which is much esteemed, called an 'Essay on Moral Statistics in France.' Perhaps you have already heard of this work, which has been noticed in your reviews. The Académie Française considered it of so much utility and importance that they bestowed on it a prize.

M. Guéry is going to England in order to continue his statistical studies: he intends to spend six months there. I think that the work which he will publish on his return will be full of interest for us, and will be no doubt of real use to the English themselves. Now that, thank God, the two countries are on good terms, they ought to endeavour to enlighten each other. I wish no better fortune for M. Guéry than to find in England as excellent a friend as I did.

I suppose that you have finished drawing up your important Report on the Poor Law. If so, I shall be much obliged if you will send me a copy through our Consul-general. The volume containing extracts from your Inquiry on the same subject has excited great interest here. The result of your labours cannot fail to be equally appreciated.

. . . . .

&c. &c. &c.
ALEXIS DE TOCQUEVILLE.

P.S.—In three months I shall publish my work upon 'American Institutions.' You may be sure that I shall send you an early copy.

Lincoln's Inn, February 17, 1835.

My dear Sir,—Pray accept my best thanks for your excellent work, 'De la Démocratie en Amérique,' which I have read with great interest, delight, and I hope instruction. It appears to me one of the most remarkable books of the age.

I am most anxious that it should be reviewed and translated here; but there is great difficulty in getting a review of any book requiring much thought. Those who are competent for such a work seldom like to write anonymously.

If, however, you will sacrifice a few copies for the chance, and will send them to me, I will put them into the hands of the editors of our principal reviews, the 'Edinburgh,' 'Quarterly,' 'Westminster,' and 'London.' I think also that it would be worth your while to send a copy to the Athenæum Club, both in order to obtain readers, and to insure your admission to that club (the best I think in London) on your arrival. The best mode of sending books to me in London is to direct to me, at M. J. B. Baillière, Libraire, 13 bis Rue de l'École de Médecine, Paris. Their parcels leave Paris for London every Saturday evening, and will come to me without any expense to you. I think too that it might be well to send (by the same means) copies to Lord Brougham and Lord Lansdowne.

A few remarks have occurred to me, principally in your second volume.

Page 58. Is not a passage omitted after the eleventh line? Perhaps the passage at p. 59, beginning 'Je regarde,' ought to be here inserted.

P. 76. Has money fallen in value in France since the Empire? It has risen everywhere else.

P. 76. *Note.* The expenditure on the poor arises not from the democratic nature of the American Government, but from the compulsory provision. In Denmark the most despotic, and England, the most aristocratic, country in Europe it is far greater than in America.

P. 115. I do not think that in England the wealth of the poor has been sacrificed to that of the rich. As far as my investigations extend, the wages of the English labourer are higher than those of any labourer. He has not landed property, because it is more profitable to him to work for another than to cultivate; but this depends on the same ground which makes it more profitable to work for a cotton manufacturer than to make stockings for his own use. It is a part of the system of the division of labour, of which la grande culture is only an instance.

P. 383. *Note.* What sort of milles carrés do you refer to? Not certainly English.

P. 393. I cannot think that population is an element of wealth. It may rather be said to be an element of poverty. The wealth or poverty of the *people* of a country depends on the proportion between their numbers and the aggregate wealth of that country. Diminish their numbers, the wealth remaining the same, and they will be, individually, richer. The people of Ireland, and indeed of England, would be richer if they were fewer. I do not call a country like China, where there is an immense population, individually poor, a rich country, though the aggregate wealth of China is greater than the aggregate wealth of Holland, where the population is, comparatively, individually rich.

I am delighted to hear that you are likely to be soon in London; and I trust to have the earliest information of your arrival.

I shall send to you to-morrow by the Ambassador's bag[1] a little pamphlet, written by me, but not avowed,

---

[1] Extracts from this pamphlet are published in Mr. Senior's *Ireland*. Longmans, 1868. The portions, however, which relate to English politics are for the most part omitted.—ED.

on National Property. It will show you the feelings of the Whig party here, as I wrote it in concurrence with some of the leaders of that party; and they have in general adopted its views.

With our best regards, believe me, my dear Sir, yours very truly,

NASSAU W. SENIOR.

Paris, February 21, 1835.

My dear Mr. Senior,—I thank you much for the kind letter which you have just sent to me. There is no one whose approbation I was more anxious to gain, and I am proud of having obtained it. How much I wish that the book could be made generally accessible to your countrymen, and that they might share your opinion. Its success here much surpasses my expectations. But I shall not be satisfied unless it extends to what I consider, in an intellectual sense, my second country. I was glad to see that I had already taken the measures for insuring publicity which you advise. I had sent copies to the 'Edinburgh,' the 'Quarterly,' and the 'Westminster,' and I thank you for your kind offer of presenting them to the editors of those reviews, begging you at the same time to give them some account of the book and to ask them to grant it an early notice. You will understand that I am anxious that it should become known before my approaching visit to England.

I shall be delighted to follow your advice by sending copies to Lord Brougham and Lord Lansdowne. I had already thought of so doing, but I confess that I was deterred by what happened to me eighteen months ago, when I sent a copy of the 'Système Pénitentiaire' to the Archbishop of Dublin with a letter of presentation. Since then I have not heard a syllable of His Grace, which has astonished me very much, for in our country there is no person so insignificant as not to expect some acknowledgment when he presents a book, or an answer when he writes a letter.

I come now to your criticisms, which have given me almost as much pleasure as your praise, because they prove the attention with which you have read my book, and, besides, I intend to make use of several of them in preparing a second edition.

You tell me that on page 58 of the second volume, a passage is misplaced. I have looked again at the passage: you are right.

A note on p. 76 induces you to ask if money has fallen in value in France since the Empire? in other words, whether more money is wanted *now* than *then* for purchasing the same things? My answer is, that I have not made any particular inquiries upon this point. I followed the current opinion on the subject. I do not understand how it can be erroneous. Although much less was produced from the mines during the civil wars in America, I cannot believe the mass of gold and silver in circulation to be less now than it was twenty years ago. However, I intend to endeavour to clear up this point as regards France.

You tell me with much truth respecting a note on p. 77, that a poor law is no proof of a republican government; but my reason for quoting America in this respect was to give French readers an instance of the expense willingly incurred by a democracy. There are many causes which may induce any government to relieve the poor at the expense of the state, but a republican government is from its nature forced to do so.

In page 115 I said that in English legislation the *bien du pauvre had in the end been sacrificed to that of the rich.* You attack me on this point, of which you certainly are a competent judge. You must allow me, however, to differ from you. In the first place, it seems to me that you give to the expression *le bien du pauvre* a confined sense which was not mine; you translate it *wealth*, a word especially applied to money. I meant by it all that contributes to happiness; personal consideration, political right, easy justice, intellectual enjoyments, and many other indirect sources of contentment. I shall believe, till I have proof of the contrary, that in England the rich have gradually monopolised almost all the advantages that society bestows upon mankind. Taking the question in your own restricted sense, and admitting that a poor man is better paid when he works on another man's land than when he cultivates his own, do you not think that there are political, moral, and intellectual advantages, which are a more than sufficient and, above all, a permanent compensation for the loss that you point out?

I know, however, that this is one of the most important questions of the age, and perhaps the one on which we differ most entirely. Soon I hope that we shall have an opportunity for discussing it. In the meanwhile I cannot help telling you how dissatisfied I was at the way in which Mr. McCulloch, whose talent, however, I acknowledge, has treated this question. I was astonished at his quoting us Frenchmen in support of his arguments in favour of the non-division of landed property; and at his asserting that the physical well-being of the people deteriorates in proportion to the sub-division of property. I am convinced that up to the present time this is substantially false. Such an opinion would find no echo here, even from those who attack the law of succession as impolitic and dangerous in its ultimate tendency. Even *they* acknowledge that *as yet* the progress of our people in comfort and civilisation has been rapid and uninterrupted, and that in these respects the France of to-day is as unlike as possible to the France of twenty years ago. I repeat, however, that such questions cannot be treated in writing. They must be reserved for long conversations.

My friend and former colleague, M. Gustave de Beaumont, has also just published a book upon America. If, as I hope, you have time to read it, I am sure that you will be pleased with it. The question of Slavery, which I could only touch upon, is treated thoroughly and with great ability in this work. M. de Beaumont hopes soon to have the honour of making your acquaintance, for he intends to accompany me to England.

&c. &c. &c.
A. DE TOCQUEVILLE.

Letter from Archbishop Whately.

Dublin, March 2, 1835.

My dear Senior,—I should have been glad to be able to send M. de Tocqueville, along with my thanks for his book, and the very flattering and gratifying letter that accompanied it, some specific remarks on the parts that should have most struck me on perusal. But I have been so incessantly harassed with business that I have not yet been able even to cut open the leaves; though I am still looking forward from day to day to an opportunity of deriving not only pleasure from it, but valuable instruction with a view to the reforms which I hope will ere long be commenced in our own system. In the meantime I ought at once to have returned my grateful acknowledgments for his present. I will beg you now to do so for me, and to apologise for a negligence which might seem unaccountable to anyone who does not actually see, and no one else can know, the variety of harassing business that besets me. Over and above all proper episcopal business, 'that which cometh upon me daily, the care of all the Churches,' I am a member of nearly thirty boards, infinitely varied in the matters pertaining to them and several of them very important and laborious.

R. DUBLIN.

Lincoln's Inn, March 5, 1835.

My dear Sir,—I send to you on the other side a copy of a letter which I have just received from the Archbishop of Dublin. You will see how it happens that you have not heard from him before.

Your copies for Lord Lansdowne and Lord Brougham reached me, and were forwarded on Tuesday last. So did M. de Beaumont's two copies of 'Marie' for the 'Quarterly' and 'Athenæum.' I have written to Lockhart, the Editor of the 'Quarterly;' and have mentioned to him your work as demanding a review. He had not then seen it.

I have read 'Marie' with great delight and instruction. It is very powerfully written, though perhaps with too much 'onction' for our colder tastes. Blanco White is preparing a review of 'la Démocratie' for the 'New London Review.'[1] He had only read the introduction when I heard from him. He says that it is the most profound view of society in Europe that he has ever seen. Dr. Bowring says that he will endeavour to have it reviewed in the 'Westminster.' But you must not be surprised if you see no reviews for two or three months. It is very difficult to get anyone to review works requiring much thought. Persons capable of doing so do not like to write anonymously. When I have the pleasure of seeing you I hope to discuss the question about 'le bien des pauvres.' I believe that, so

---

[1] The *New London Review* was started in 1829, under the editorship of Blanco White. See J. H. Newman's Essays, vol. i. p. 27.—ED.

far as they are in a worse situation here than in the rest of Europe (which is seldom, perhaps never, the case) it has arisen solely from the misguided benevolence of the aristocracy; and through an abuse of the poor laws. In Scotland, the most aristocratic portion of Great Britain, they are remarkably well off.

Pray say to M. de Beaumont with how much pleasure I look forward to his acquaintance.

Yours very truly,
N. W. SENIOR.

March 14, 1835.

My dear Mr. Senior,—A thousand thanks for the steps you have taken respecting the English Reviews. I hope that they will produce some fruits. I do not, however, conceal from myself that in a country agitated as yours is at present, the curiosity of the public is little directed towards subjects of general and external interest, such as those of which my book treats.

A scientific society in my province has asked me lately for a paper on Pauperism. I have begun it, but in order to finish it I ought to know what is going on in England, and particularly the New Poor Law, which was passed I think last year. Would it be possible for you to send me the Act of Parliament? you would render me a great service, especially if it came soon.

I received the other day an extremely kind letter from Lord Lansdowne, for which I am very grateful.

. . . .

A. DE TOCQUEVILLE.

P.S.—I hope that when my visit to London takes place, the Archbishop of Dublin will have already arrived there, and that I shall have the pleasure of seeing him. Meantime pray remember me to him.

March 18, 1835.

My dear Sir,—I have directed two more pamphlets to be sent by the Ambassador's bag. I cannot guess through whose fault the one already sent has miscarried. I have also directed a copy of the Poor Law Act, and of a preface of mine explaining it, to be sent. They will I hope go to-morrow. I had also directed copies of the Report of the Poor Law Commissioners, and of the Extracts of their evidence, and of Messrs. Cowell's and Wrottesley's reports, addressed to the Commissioners, to be forwarded to you. But they are too large for the bag, and I have not found any other opportunity.

On consulting with my French bookseller, Baillière, he has reminded me that I sent copies of these three volumes to his brother, the bookseller at Paris, and that your best way will be to call there and take them from him, and I will, as soon as there is an opportunity, send him fresh ones. If you will do this, you will, I hope, find them ready for you, as Baillière has promised to write immediately to his brother on the subject.

The three volumes are

1. Report of the Commissioners to the King.
2. Extracts of their evidence.
3. A small volume containing reports by Cowell, Cameron, and Wrottesley to the Commissioners.

The report, or at least three-fourths of it, was written by me, and all that was not written by me was re-written by me. The greater part of the Act, founded on it, was also written by me; and in fact I am responsible for the effects, good or evil (and they must be one or the other in an enormous degree), of the whole measure.

When you are here I will show you the evidence in full. It fills fourteen folio volumes.

Ever yours,
N. W. SENIOR.

London, May 1835.

My dear Sir,—Not being able to call on you to-day, M. de Beaumont and I desire to express our thanks, first for the books which you have been so kind as to send to us, and likewise for the letter which we have just received from the Athenæum. Allow me also to tell you with what keen interest we read the political pamphlet which accompanied the book. For my part I have not read anything for many years throwing so much light upon the state of the country and the position of parties. I consider this pamphlet, and M. de Beaumont shares my opinion, as the most valuable document which could fall into the hands of a foreigner visiting England for the purpose of studying its peculiarities and completing his political education.

I am, &c.,
A. DE TOCQUEVILLE.

Lincoln's Inn, November 20, 1835.

My dear Sir,—The bearer of this note is Mr. Burnley of Trinidad, an old friend of mine, and the brother-in-law of Mr. Hume.

He is anxious to make, or rather renew, his acquaintance with you. I say renew, because he once went over one of the American prisons in your company.

I can give you little public news since your departure. The New Poor Law Bill is working admirably, and if the Report of the new Commissioners is out in time I will send it to you as a proof of our progress.

Your work on America is exciting every day more and more attention. You have probably seen an excellent review of it, by John Mill, in the 'London Review.'

Our Government[1] is timid, afraid of O'Connell, afraid of Sir Robert Peel, afraid of the King; but yet I believe likely to last. The general prosperity of the country is an element in its favour not easily counterbalanced. And it is beyond all comparison the most honest administration that we have ever had. Much more so than a Tory administration can possibly be, since it believes whatever progress it makes in reform to be beneficial; whereas a Tory minister believes all the progress which is forced on him to be mischievous.

When you have leisure I look forward to hearing that you are well and well employed in France, and with still

---

[1] Lord Melbourne was Prime Minister.—ED.

more pleasure, to hearing that you are going to pay us another visit.

Believe me, my dear Sir, yours very truly,

NASSAU W. SENIOR.

Paris, January 27, 1836.

My dear Mr. Senior,—Your letter dated November 20 reached me only eight or ten days ago, Mr. Burnley not having delivered it earlier. I received that gentleman as well as I could, but much less hospitably than I wished. I had, unfortunately, only too good an excuse for this. I have just had the misfortune of losing my mother; and you will feel that in the first moment of the grief caused by this sad event, I was not in a fit state to do the honours of Paris to a stranger. Happily Mr. Burnley proposes to spend the whole winter here, and I intend to do all I can to make myself agreeable to him. I am all the more sanguine as to my powers, as I have now an excellent interpreter. You are doubtless aware that three months ago I married a countrywoman of yours, and I rejoice in telling you that I every day find fresh reasons for congratulating myself on my choice.

Thank you very much for the details you give me as to your home politics. It seems that with you the Revolution, taking the word in the sense of a tranquil progress, is still going on; or rather the Revolution seems to me to have been accomplished on the day when you introduced the most democratic class into the Electoral Body. The rest is only a consequence.

With us, for the moment at least, all things seem completely restored to their normal state. With the exception of agriculture, which is suffering a little, everything prospers in an astonishing manner. For the first time for five years the idea of stability seems to have entered men's minds, and with it the desire for commercial enterprise. The almost feverish activity which has always characterised us is leaving the domain of politics for that of material well-being. If I am not greatly mistaken, we shall see during the next few years immense progress in this direction. But the Government would be very wrong to over-rate the consequences of this happy state of affairs.

The nation has suffered horribly; she is now luxuriating in the repose which has at length been granted to her. But all our past experience teaches us that this repose may itself become fatal to the Government. In proportion as the fatigue of these latter years is less felt, we shall see political passion restored to life, and if whilst it is strong the Government does not redouble its prudence and treat with great circumspection the susceptibilities of the country, some day a sudden storm will burst upon its head; but will it ever understand this? I doubt.

You saw the laws it proposed last year against the Press,—laws as odious as they were unnecessary, and of which the sole result would have been to restore the power of the Press if they had been carried into effect. But the same things are written now as formerly, because license in writing has become a habit with us, and habits are more powerful than laws.

At present the great question with us is the conversion of the funds. The opposition proceeds from the King himself, who expressed himself so strongly in the Council against this financial measure; that ministers have been forced to assume an attitude which they cannot any longer sustain.

The majority in the Chambers, which in reality, as I have often told you, serves the passions of the Government only when it shares them, has eagerly proclaimed itself in favour of the measure. No doubt it will gain the day, nevertheless I do not think that the measure will pass this year. . . . .

A. DE TOCQUEVILLE.

Paris, January 11, 1837.

My dear Mr. Senior,—I did not reach Paris until the end of December, and received only two days ago your Report on the Poor Laws and the Treatise on Political Economy, which you were so kind as to send me by Mr. Greg. A thousand thanks to you for having thought of me. You could not have given me anything that I should have liked better than your outline of Political Economy. I have often confessed to you that I was insufficiently informed on this important portion of human science, and I have many times thought that you were the man most capable of supplying this deficiency. All that you publish is much valued by me, but especially what you write on political economy.

VOL. I.   C

I have not yet, however, been able to read what you have sent. I am, at this moment, so wrapped up in my second work on America, that I scarcely see or hear what is going on around me. I think that my book will be finished in the summer, and published next autumn. I do not know if it will be good; but I can affirm that I cannot make it better. I devote to it all my time and all my intelligence.

Our ministry is still *in a dubious state*.[1] Its downfall does not appear to be imminent, but it may happen at any moment in consequence of the most trifling question; for the majority in the Chamber may be said rather to suffer the ministers to exercise the functions of government than to entrust them with its responsibilities. It would have a still worse chance if it were not for M. Molé, who attracts many members naturally hostile to the theorists.[2] The material prosperity of the country is still very great and increases slowly but steadily; if we are able to preserve peace and our institutions, even in their present imperfect state, for twenty years longer, the internal aspect of France will be entirely metamorphosed.

⁎ ⁎ ⁎ ⁎ ⁎ ⁎

A. DE TOCQUEVILLE.

Kensington, February 15, 1838.

My dear Sir,—Mr. Ellice, who has distinguished himself among our diplomatists and administrators, is on

---

[1] *Sic* in Original.—ED.
[2] *Doctrinaires* is the French expression.—ED.

his way to Paris, and is very anxious to have the honour of making your acquaintance. I have ventured therefore to give him this note of introduction; and I have begged him to take charge of two little works of mine which may not yet have reached you; one of them indeed—the Instructions to Assistant Commissioners in the Handloom Inquiry—is not yet published, and what I send is only the proof. It may serve as a specimen of the inquiries which we are instituting as to the state of the labouring population.

I was delighted to find from the note which I had the honour of receiving from you last summer, that you were then busily engaged on your work on American Manners. It is a great happiness that such a subject should have fallen into such hands.

I shall be very anxious to hear of its completion, and still more so if I hear that the termination of your labours is likely to enable you to revisit England.

I am thinking myself, if I can escape for a fortnight, of making, in the beginning of April, a short tour in Normandy with Lord Shelburne, Lord Lansdowne's now only remaining son. I fear, however, that there is no chance of your being at that time in the country.

Mrs. Senior begs me to present to you her compliments, and to say how anxious she is to renew her acquaintance with you, and to make that of Madame de Tocqueville.

With our united regards, believe me, my dear Sir, yours very truly,

N. W. SENIOR.

Château de Baugy, February 29, 1838.

The post has this instant brought me, my dear Mr. Senior, the letter of which Mr. Ellice was the bearer, and which he could not deliver in person as I have been away from Paris for some months, and shall continue to be so for some months longer.

I sincerely regret that I was not able to make the acquaintance of Mr. Ellice, whose name, I need not say, was well known to me. Pray tell him how eagerly I should have sought and cultivated his society if I had been in Paris. I would myself write to him to express my regret if I knew his address.

I hope, my dear Mr. Senior, that you will feel a great admiration for me when you hear that I have torn myself away from the charms of Paris, and of the whole political and literary world fermenting there, in order to shut myself up with my books, pens, and paper in the midst of forests almost as dense as those of the New World and much less poetical.

I could find no other way of finishing the book at which I have been working almost incessantly for the last three years, and in spite of this effort I am not yet quite sure of completing it, as I want to do, by the middle of the summer.

The subject is much more difficult and infinitely wider than I supposed when I undertook its treatment. I should probably have recoiled from the task had I been aware of its extent.

I am staying here with one of my brothers, far enough

from Paris to enjoy perfect liberty, but near enough to take a holiday there from time to time and fetch the books I require. I am leading a busy, monotonous, but very agreeable life, so do not pity me too much.

Allow me to tell you that it is a very mistaken idea on your part to think of taking a pleasure trip in Normandy in the month of April. Do you not know France is of all countries the one where you most require a bright sun to make you forget the bad inns? You should instead pay a little visit to Paris, and let me know beforehand. I should certainly join you there, for I feel an intense desire for some conversation with you. I should also be very glad to make acquaintance with Lord Lansdowne's son. Pray remember me particularly to his father.

. . . .

A. DE TOCQUEVILLE.

[Two letters follow asking for information on the measures taken by England for the emancipation of slaves. They consist merely of questions. I am sorry to say that Mr. Senior's answers were not among the letters returned to me.—ED.]

Masters' Offices, Southampton Buildings, February 27, 1841.

My dear Sir,—I take advantage of the privilege of General Hamilton to send to you a copy of a Report on Handloom Weavers, which I printed a few days ago, after having given to it the leisure of nearly two years. If you can find time to look through it, you will find that it treats at some length many important questions.

During the course of the last two months I have read through, not for the first or even the second time, your great work. Will you allow me to offer to you the following observations?

You appear to consider France as eminently democratic, England as eminently aristocratic. And yet many of the qualities which you describe as marking democratic societies appear to belong to us much more than to you.

For instance, the desire for *bien-être*. In England the desire to make and increase a fortune seems to me to urge many more people, and more constantly and forcibly, than in France. A French tradesman spends much more of his time and of his money on amusement and dress than an English one; he retires much sooner from business, satisfied with his fortune. I believe that next to the United States there is no population so sedulously intent on fortune as the English and Scotch.

Take again individualism. Except on questions affecting religious opinions and religious feelings, such as Church questions, slavery, or slave trade, little interest is felt in politics by the English people.

No ordinances of the Crown would produce in London barricades or insurrection. Probably there are not one hundred people out of London who have taken the pains to know where Ghilzie is, or what has been the nature of the Indian war, in which an empire is supposed to have been conquered.¹ The Eastern question, which you thought and think so much of, has never elicited with us the least interest, except so far as we have feared that it might bring war. Whether Mehemet Ali reigned in Constantinople and Alexandria, or Mahmoud in both these countries, not two persons out of London, and not ten persons in London, care one sixpence. Lord Palmerston has not acquired a grain of popularity by his success. The only remark is, 'We wish he would keep quiet.'

Again you say that a democratic nation is pacific, an aristocratic one warlike. Now nothing, I fear, is more warlike than the feeling in France, nothing is more pacific than the feeling in England. All that we require from our foreign minister is, to keep peace. Lord Palmerston's only defence is, that he thought he used the best means to avoid war. He never thought of defending himself by saying that he was anxious to extend English influence, or by any appeals to the desire of national aggrandisement; for he knows that we have no such desire.

The speech which you addressed to the French Chamber would have been utterly ruinous to any English statesman. What, it would have been said, to think of going to war merely to prevent our being excluded from taking part in the affairs of Syria or Egypt? or to show that we are not unable to go to war? Or because, we, being one, are, in a business taken up by the five Powers, required to yield to the opinion of the four? Now you laid down to the French Chamber these three

---

¹ The war in Cabul and Affghanistan.—ED.

cases as fit causes of war. In the English House, either of Lords or Commons, we should consider such proposals as scarcely deserving a serious answer. The passage which you struck out of the Address—namely, that *if you were attacked* you would resist, forms the groundwork of all English feeling on peace and war.

Will you let me add some politico-economical remarks?

In vol. iv. p. 51, you appear to consider the rate of wages as affected by other causes than those to which I have been accustomed to refer it. I have always been accustomed to consider wages as governed by the comparative supply of labour on the one hand, and of capital on the other, and by the productiveness of labour. Where the capital, in proportion to the number of labourers is large, and the labour is productive, wages are high, because the labourer produces much, and has a large share of what he produces. This is the case in our manufacturing towns. Where the capital is large, but the labour is comparatively unproductive, as in our best agricultural counties, the labourer gets less. Where the capital is small, and the labour also unproductive, as in Ireland, he gets still less. It does not seem to me that the institutions of a country (except slavery or serfage) have anything to do with the matter.

P. 291. You appear to consider public debts as *capital.* It must be recollected that the capital of a public debt has been all spent. It may be a sort of capital in the hands of a public *creditor,* but certainly the obligation to pay is not capital.

P. 295. We have no exceptional tribunals.

P. 299. As the desire for railroads, &c. increases, so, with us, does the power of creating them by associations. The Government does not interfere. Believe me, my dear Sir, yours ever truly,

N. W. SENIOR.

[A short note of introduction is omitted here.— ED.]

London, May 10, 1842.

My dear M. de Tocqueville,—M. Ritter duly presented himself, dined with us one day, but two days afterwards wrote to say that, finding his ignorance of English an obstacle in London, he had retired for six months to the country. On his return I hope he will be *bi-linguis*, and I have no doubt that the honour of an introduction from you will enable him to establish himself. A wish to understand German is rapidly extending itself, and his general knowledge will enable him to teach it philosophically.

I fear there is not much chance of our meeting in Paris. August, September, and October, the months in which I can be absent from England, are those in which Paris is empty, always excepting the hotels, which are full while all the other habitations are deserted. This circumstance, added to the absence of steam communications, and some troublesome regulations as to carriages and passports, have made me in general prefer the Rhine as the access to the Continent. But is there no chance of your visiting England? or of our meeting in Germany or Switzerland or Italy?

I should be delighted indeed if your path and ours should coincide. We pursued your steps, as I found by the Visitors' book, in 1838 for a considerable time, though we never overtook you.

While I am writing this letter your *discours* has been forwarded to me. I had already read it, with the delight and instruction which it has afforded to everyone here. And I am proud that you have honoured me with a copy *ex dono*.

If M. de St. Aulaire is not alarmed at the size of the packet, I shall venture to accompany this note by four brochures of mine. Two are on our English Poor Laws, a matter from which I cannot extricate myself, and the other two on our financial measures of 1841 and 1842.

The remarks by a Guardian contain (p. 2), a passage not intended for French eyes, which I will beg you to consider as not sent to you. With our united best regards, believe me, my dear M. de Tocqueville, ever yours truly,

N. W. SENIOR.

I hear a rumour of your coming to England. I trust there is some foundation for it.

Paris, December 14, 1842.

My dear Mr. Senior,—I have been occupied lately in studying with reference to our political affairs a great constitutional question which must have arisen and been discussed in England.

The manner in which you may have treated and

decided it cannot fail to exercise great influence upon my opinion. I think I cannot do better than to apply to you for information. This is the question:

You are aware that last year M. Guizot signed a treaty[1] which the Chamber prevented him from ratifying. Was the Chamber right or wrong? this is a point which it is unnecessary and which it would take too long to examine. All that I want to know is, whether, such being the case, according to your constitutional principles the result would or would not be the resignation of the ministers who had signed the treaty. I fancy that there must have been precedents in your constitutional history, at any rate the question must have been discussed in works upon public and political law. It is quite new in France, and on this account as much as for the sake of its practical importance, I have a great wish to study it thoroughly. If you can assist me you will render me a real service.

I should be much obliged if you could give me an early answer. I am naturally desirous of forming a definite opinion before the beginning of the session, which will be on the 9th of next month, because, in the first place, it is possible that the question may be debated; and, secondly, because when once the session is opened, it is impossible to study anything consecutively. Again, forgive my importunity; my excuse is the motive which induces me to apply to you. I should not do so

---

[1] The treaty for the suppression of the slave trade—signed December 20, 1841—ratified by Austria, Great Britain, Prussia, and Russia, February 19, 1842—never ratified by France. See Guizot, *Mémoires pour servir, &c.*, vol. vi. p. 130, *et seq.*—ED.

did I not believe that from your information and your talents you were of all my English acquaintance the most capable of enlightening me.

A. DE TOCQUEVILLE.

London, December 20, 1842.

My dear M. de Tocqueville,—I have always hitherto been delighted to hear from you and to answer you; but I am less so this time, as I fear some portion of what I must say may appear unfriendly or presumptuous.

I do not believe that a parallel case to M. Guizot's has ever occurred in England or ever could occur. An English minister finding a treaty signed by his ambassador, after a negotiation in which the ambassador had not exceeded his powers, would have felt himself bound, for the sake of his own honour or for the honour of his country, to ratify it. And would have done so, even in the case—also I think an impossible one—of the House or Houses of Parliament declaring their disapprobation. He would have said, This is an executive, not a legislative act, and I must ratify it, whatever be the consequence. Cases certainly have occurred, though rarely, of treaties signed, and not ratified, in other countries. But it has been either in absolute monarchies, where the king is in fact the minister, or in those constitutional countries, such as America, in which a treaty is a legislative, not an executive act. In America too the President is the minister, and he never resigns.

I think, therefore, that you will find no precedent, and no discussion on the subject.

But assuming the possibility of an English minister being in M. Guizot's position, would he now resign? I think not, according to our *present* feelings. I say our *present* feelings, for since the Reform Act a great change has taken place in public opinion on this subject.

Formerly, when the adverse parties were really only adverse personal factions, a minister used to resign at the first check. It was considered one of the rules of the game that he should do so. And it was a convenient rule, since it enabled the party in power to rule absolutely, and kept up the interest of the game by a frequent change of ministers.

But now politics are not a game but a business. A change of ministry is now a national event, and a minister feels himself bound to remain in office as long as the majority of the House of Commons desire that he should do so. The example was set by Peel in 1835, and followed, indeed improved on, by his successors.

An English minister in M. Guizot's position would say, 'I have been defeated in a measure which I think right, but the Chamber still confides in me, and while it does so, I remain at my post. If you think that I have lost the confidence of the Chamber, put that question to the vote; but while you fear to take that step I will continue minister.'

So much for politics.

Indeed I most earnestly wish that I could have the pleasure of seeing you again. But unfortunately at the times when I can best quit England (August, September, and October) you are never in Paris. And this circumstance, joined to the absence of railroads and steamboats, has made me turn my steps rather towards Germany than France. Is there any chance of our meeting abroad? Next autumn we remain in England, but in 1844 we shall be in Bohemia, Silesia, and Saxony.

Ever yours truly,
N. W. SENIOR.

February 12, 1844.

My dear Mr. Senior,—I did not answer your letter immediately, because I did not wish to do so until I had read your pamphlet,[1] and the excitement of our parliamentary debates did not allow me to read it for a long time.

I have just finished it, and I can assure you that I have never read anything on the subject of Ireland which has appeared to me more worthy of the consideration of statesmen.

It would be impossible to put a more complete and striking picture into a smaller frame.

Most of the things you say are, as you yourself remark, already known. Nothing new can, in fact, be said upon a subject which has for so many years attracted the attention of the whole world, and has been studied by so many eminent men.

---

[1] An article in the *Edinburgh Review* for January 1844, re-published in Mr. Senior's *Ireland*. Longmans, 1868. —ED.

But you have succeeded so well in bringing out the chief features of this immense and confused picture that it seems as if one saw it for the first time in your pages.

As for the remedies you propose, a great deal might be said about them; even a long letter would be insufficient to discuss them. I would rather wait for the opportunity, which I hope soon to have, of conversing with you.

The announcement that you are coming soon gives me great pleasure. This is not the first time that I have told you of the value I set on your friendship, and on the pleasure and instruction I derive from your conversation.

You will meet here many who share my opinion, and a great many more who earnestly wish to know you.

You ask for my advice as to your journey. Here it is: I think that your best plan would be to go to Havre. From Havre to Rouen there is a very agreeable mode of transport by steam-boat, and a quick land journey. When once you have reached Rouen, the railroad takes you to Paris in four hours.

I am, &c.,
A. DE TOCQUEVILLE.

[There is a gap here in the correspondence.—ED.]

To N. W. Senior, Esq.

Tocqueville, August 25, 1847.

Many thanks for your route; not that I hope to fall in with you in Italy, but because I hope to be able to meet you in Paris. I shall be delighted to see you again after so long an absence, and to talk over with you all that has been going on, and is going on in the world. You will find France calm and not unprosperous, but anxious. Men's minds have been subject for some time to a strange uneasiness. In the midst of tranquillity more profound than any that we have enjoyed for a very long time, the idea that our present position is unstable besets them. As for myself, though not without alarm, I am less anxious; I do not exaggerate our danger. I believe that our social edifice will continue to rest on its present basis, because no one, even if he wish to change its foundation, can point out another. But yet the state of public feeling disturbs me.

The middle classes, cajoled and bribed for the last seventeen years by the Government, have gradually assumed towards the rest of the nation the position of a little aristocracy, and without its higher feelings: one feels ashamed of being led by such a vulgar and corrupt aristocracy, and if this feeling should prevail among the lower classes it may produce great calamities.

And yet how can a Government be prevented from using corruption, when the nature of our constituencies makes corruption so convenient, and our centralisation makes it so easy? The fact is that we are trying an experiment of which I cannot foresee the result. We are trying to employ at the same time two instruments which, I believe, have never been combined before: an elected Assembly and a highly centralised Executive. It is the greatest problem of modern times. We have proposed it to the world, but it has not yet been solved.

I am anxious for your inferences from what you have seen in Germany, and are now seeing in Italy. Kind and affectionate regards.

A. DE TOCQUEVILLE.

Splügen, September 30, 1847.

My dear M. de Tocqueville,—I have not ventured to write to you while I was on the other side of the Alps, as I know from experience that it is not safe to form plans depending on their being passable—but now, having left the formidable Splügen behind me, I can say that we shall be in Paris on October 12. I have written to engage rooms at the Hôtel Wagram, Rue de Rivoli. We take the route of the Rhine and Brussels, and certainly the first thing I do in Paris will be to go to the Rue de la Madeleine.

I must own that the great difficulty in France appears to me the weakness, almost the want, of the aristocratic element in your Government. We perhaps have too much of it—though it is so rapidly diminishing that perhaps I ought rather to say we *had* too much.

On the other hand, you seem to me to have too much

of the monarchical element. We have succeeded in reducing the Crown to a mere ceremony. Our queen is a phantom, put there not to act, but merely to fill space; to prevent anyone else from being there.

We have spent a month in the north of Italy, in the Austrian dominions. It is a melancholy country. Everywhere there are the traces of a civilisation which exceeded what now exists. I am glad to get out of it, and leave behind me fine bad inns, begging children, and a peasantry in rags, but handsomer than the higher orders.

Ever yours,
N. W. SENIOR.

[We spent a pleasant fortnight in Paris in October, enjoying the society of M. de Tocqueville and of some of our other friends; but at that time Mr. Senior kept no notes of his travels.

In the following February the Revolution took place. Mr. Senior's account of the events which led to it and of the crisis itself precedes the journals kept in France and Italy. The letter to which the following is an answer is not among those returned to me.—ED.]

Paris, April 10, 1848.

My dear Mr. Senior,—I was away when your letter came. I found it on my return only three days ago. I immediately went to Mr. Austin's, to know what had prevented your visit to Paris. I was grieved to hear that your health had forced you to change your plans.

I am doubly sorry not to see you, on account of the cause. I had been the more anxious for your arrival as I expected to have derived from your conversation some ideas which would have been of special value at this juncture in our affairs.

It has not escaped your notice that our greatest evils are not the result of fierce political excitement, but of the frightful ignorance of the masses as to the real conditions of production and of social prosperity. Our sufferings are caused less by false ideas on politics properly so called, than by false notions on political economy.

I do not think that a poor-law such as you suggest would, at least at present, remedy the evil. The Revolution was not brought about by the privations of the working classes. In some districts they certainly suffered from want, but in general, I may say that in no other country or period had the working classes been better off than they were in France. This was especially true of those who were employed in agriculture. There the labourer did not need work, but work needed labourers. In consequence of the sub-division of landed property, there was a deficiency of hands. The crisis from which the workmen in large manufactories were suffering, lasted a very short time, and though severe was not unexampled. It was not want, but ideas, that brought about that violent subversion; chimerical ideas on the relations between labour and capital, extravagant theories as to the degree in which the Government might interfere between the working man and the employer, doctrines of ultra-centralisation which had at last persuaded large numbers that it depended on the State not only to save them from want but to place them in easy comfortable circumstances. You must feel that to these diseased imaginations a poor-law would not be an efficient remedy. I am far, however, from saying that recourse must not be had to it. I even think that the people ought long ago to have obtained one; but this law would not be enough to extricate us from our present difficulties, for, I repeat, we have to contend with ideas rather than with wants.

Three weeks before the Revolution, I made a speech [1] which was taken down at the time in short-hand, and

---

[1] This was the passage in M. de Tocqueville's speech on January 27, 1848 :—' It is supposed,' said he, 'that there is no danger because there is no collision. It is said, that as there is no actual disturbance of the surface of society, revolution is far off.

'Gentlemen, allow me to tell you, that I believe you deceive yourselves. Without doubt the disorder does not break out in overt acts, but it has sunk deeply into the minds of the people. Look at what is passing in the breasts of the working classes, as yet, I own, tranquil. It is true that they are not now inflamed by purely political passions in the same degree as formerly ; but do you not observe that their passions from political have become social? Do you not see gradually pervading them opinions and ideas, whose object is not merely to overthrow a law, a ministry, or even a dynasty, but society itself? to shake the very foundations on which it now rests? Do you not listen to their perpetual cry? Do you not hear incessantly repeated, that all those above them are incapable and unworthy of governing them ? that the present distribution of wealth in the world is unjust, that property rests upon no equitable basis? and do you not believe that when such opinions take root, when they spread till they have almost become general, when they penetrate deeply into the masses, that they must lead sooner or later, I know not when, I know not how, but that sooner or later they must lead to the most formidable revolutions ?

'Such, Gentlemen, is my deep conviction. I believe that at the present moment we are slumbering on a volcano; of this I am thoroughly convinced.'
—Ed.

reproduced in the 'Moniteur.' I have just had it printed exactly as it stands in the 'Moniteur.' I send you a copy; pray read it; you will see that though I knew not how or when a revolution would take place, the proximity of such an event was clearly manifest to me. I have often been reminded of this speech, which aroused at the time violent murmurs in the Chamber, from those who are now willing to own that they were wrong, and that I was right. I believed that I pointed out, as much as was possible in half an hour, the primary and deeply seated causes of that revolution. All my recent experience has had the effect of confirming me in the same opinions.

The great and real cause of the Revolution was the detestable spirit which animated the Government during this long reign; a spirit of trickery, of baseness, and of bribery, which has enervated and degraded the middle classes, destroyed their public spirit, and filled them with a selfishness so blind as to induce them to separate their interests entirely from those of the lower classes whence they sprang, which consequently have been abandoned to the counsels of men who, under pretence of serving the lower orders, have filled their heads with false ideas.

This is the root of the matter, all the rest were accidents, strange and violent in themselves, I confess, but still insufficient to produce alone such an effect. Consider, on the one hand, the causes which I have pointed out, and on the other our system of centralisation, which makes the fate of France depend on a single blow struck in Paris, and you will have the explanation of the Revolution of 1848, such as one day it will appear in history, and as I myself intend to write it if God preserves my life. Will you be so good as to present a copy of my speech to Lord Lansdowne, and remember me particularly to him?

I have alluded only to the past in this letter; to treat of the *future* more than a letter would be required.

We are in the most extraordinary position that a great nation has ever been thrown into. We are forced to witness great misfortunes; we are surrounded by great dangers. My chief hope is in the lower orders. They are deficient in intelligence, but they have instincts which are worthy of all admiration. I am myself astonished, and a foreigner would be even more surprised, to see how strong a feeling for order and true patriotism prevails: to see their good sense in all things of which they are capable of judging, and in all matters on which they have not been deceived by the ambitious dreamers to whom they were abandoned.

Adieu, dear Senior, &c.
A. DE TOCQUEVILLE.

Paris, April 17, 1848.

My dear Mr. Senior,—I received with great pleasure the papers you sent to me. They are very valuable to me, as indeed everything is which comes from you.

I have not yet been able to call upon Mr. Rogers. In these troubled times one cannot command a moment.

Émeute of April 16.

During the whole of yesterday I had a musket instead of a pen in my hand. However, the day went off capitally, and would have been decisive if the moderate party had a man of action at its head. The violent party tried to get up an insurrection. The news which reached them from the departments announcing the certain triumph of the moderate party in the elections showed the necessity for striking a blow in Paris.

Yesterday, therefore, an experiment was tried for overturning the Provisional Government. 30,000 or 40,000 workmen assembled in the Champs de Mars. The drum was immediately beaten in Paris.

In half an hour more than 100,000 National Guards were under arms. Battalions were formed in an instant and ran to the Hôtel de Ville crying, 'Long live the Provisional Government!' 'Down with the Communists!' At the end of an hour Paris was in their hands, and the mob, after vainly attempting to enter the Hôtel de Ville, dispersed.

This is the first decisive victory which has been gained by the moderate party for the last two months. God grant that they may understand how to derive from it all the advantages which it may afford!

I am glad to hear that you have resumed your project of visiting us. All who, like you, are interested in witnessing the great dramas presented from time to time by human affairs, should come to Paris. I shall be much obliged if you will bring me some documents which I think will be very useful at this juncture.

1. First, relating to the *regulation* of the House of

Commons, i.e. all the rules followed by the House in conducting its business.

We probably could learn much from it for the regulation of our Assembly.

2. In the second place, I want some papers containing information as to your income tax.

We shall not be able to avoid a similar tax, and we are anxious to know how it is imposed and collected in your country.

To explain: I wish to know how it is imposed, according to what rules, what is the cost of collection, how much it has lately produced, what effects, economical or others, it has caused, and what are the exemptions?

I shall write no more as I am extremely busy I leave Paris to-day for Normandy for the elections. I shall be back in ten days.

A. DE TOCQUEVILLE.

[A proposal made by M. Wolowski in the Chamber of Deputies to consider the prayer of the Polish delegates asking the assistance of France in restoring the independence of their country, had an effect which had never been anticipated by the distinguished speaker.

It was the pretext for a Red conspiracy. On May 15, a violent attack was made on the Assembly. A body of workmen marched along the Boulevards towards the Place de la Concorde, where they were met by a small detachment of National Guards quite inadequate to resist them. Nor was any opposition offered to their progress by a body of 1,000 Gardes Mobiles posted in front of the Assembly. The rioters rushed into the Chamber, imposed the reading of their petition on the members, and carried everything in their own way till a large detachment of National Guards under the command of General Clément Thomas came to the rescue.

Barbès and the other ringleaders marched to the Hôtel de Ville, where they proclaimed themselves a provisional government. Towards six o'clock Lamartine, accompanied by a strong body of National Guards, penetrated into the Hôtel de Ville, arrested Barbès, Albert, and their colleagues, and consigned them to Vincennes.

These were the events which induced Mr. Senior to write his first journal in May, 1848.—ED.]

CONVERSATIONS.

Extract from Mr. Senior's Journal.

Friday, May 16.—I drank tea this evening with the Tocquevilles. He attaches more importance to the events of yesterday than was given to them at the Embassy.

The cry, he said, of 'Vive la Pologne!' pronounced by 20,000 voices as they approached the Chamber, 'cette voix colossalle' as he called it, was the most formidable sound that he ever heard. He does not believe that Barbès and his companions had fully concerted their plan, otherwise their success would have been much greater.

Their entrance into the Assembly they *had* planned. Courtais, the commander of the National Guard, and Caussidière, the Préfet de Paris, were in the plot. They placed persons in whom they could confide at the entrance in the Rue de Bourgogne, and ordered them to let in the assailants. When they were in, the plan of Barbès was to force the Chamber either to pass his four decrees of war, the contribution of a milliard by the rich, the forbidding the rappel being beaten to summon the National Guards, and the punishment of 'hors la loi' against anyone who should commit violence against the people (that is, resist the mob), or refuse to pass them. For this purpose he wished the mob to retire, and leave the Chamber to obey or refuse.

If they obeyed, they became, as the Convention became after a similar obedience, the slaves of the mob. If they refused, he intended to take down the names of all who refused, declare them 'hors la loi,' and probably have them massacred.

But in the first place, he could not get his followers to quit the Chamber. And in the second place, he could not get them to keep silence for an interval sufficient to enable him formally to put the question on his decrees.

There were among the mob perhaps fifty persons, each of whom wanted to be the hero of the day. So they spent three hours in fighting (literally in fighting), said Tocqueville, for the possession of the tribune, and for the right to speak from it, while the members remained silent on their seats, taking no part whatever in the proceedings. This, it seems, was pre-arranged; the probability of an attack had been foreseen, and a passive resistance determined on.

'In the meantime,' said Tocqueville, 'the danger became greater and greater, as hour after hour elapsed without anybody coming to our assistance, and I feared every minute that the mob would become silent from fatigue, and that then Barbès would be able to force us to act. So that it was with the utmost delight that at length I heard the drum of the National Guard, and the sound of men marching in quick time in the passage.'

I asked him how he accounted for the long delay of the rescue, when there were 40,000 of their friends round the building.

He could account for it only by the great difficulty of communicating with them from within—there being few exits from the Chamber, and all of them blocked up by the mob—and by the circumstance that Courtais, the commander in chief of the Guard, had ordered those among them on whom he could rely to assist the mob, and had left the rest without any orders at all.

It is certain, however, that the situation of the Assembly was known to some persons long before the rescue—the body whom I met in the Place de la Concorde beating the rappel knew it and so did those who ran to cheer them.

Yet this was about two o'clock, and the Chamber was not rescued till about a quarter to five. The rush of

Barbès and his friends from the Chamber to the Hôtel de Ville, as soon as the rescue came, seems to have been a blind imitation of the march of the Revolutionists from the Chamber to the Hôtel de Ville on February 24. The only difference being, that then all Paris was for them, and this time it was all against them. They were pursued by 100,000 men, as I saw from the terrace of the Tuileries.

'Le peuple,' said Tocqueville, 'les a pris dans sa main immense, et les a étouffés.'

I asked where was Lamartine.

'It is not known,' said Tocqueville; 'he disappeared when the mob rushed in, and was not seen again till the rescue came.'

It is supposed that he was in one of the rooms of the Palace.

I asked Tocqueville, who hopes little from the Assembly, why it need work worse than the National Assembly of 1789, of which the members were still more numerous, and equally inexperienced?

He answered, 'Because then we had the cream of France, now we have only the skim milk. The members of the late ministerial party cannot show themselves. We of the opposition party have been re-elected, indeed, by great majorities, but we are suspected with truth of being Monarchists. We cannot take any lead in the Chamber. The Legitimists, of whom there are about 120, are naturally objects of still greater suspicion. So we leave the field to the 680 merchants, lawyers, and proprietors, whom the Provinces have sent to us, timid, pacific, well-intentioned men, but quite new to public business.'

Thursday, May 25.—I went to pay a visit to Thiers, who came to Paris yesterday. I found him, however, so busy with electioneering that I could have little conversation with him, and as he goes this evening we shall not meet again. He begged me, which is significant, to send him a collection of Poor-law documents.

Afterwards I called on Madame de Tocqueville.

I told her that I had left Thiers electioneering. She feared that he would come into the Assembly, in which his powers of speaking and experience would give him great power, which he would use in attacking the present Government, without being able to form one himself.

In the evening I dined with the Tocquevilles. The guests were Cousin, Molé, Beaumont, and a deputy whose name I forget, with his wife.

The dinner was very gay. Cousin, who put me much in mind of Lord Brougham, took the lead. We talked of Thiers, and the general opinion agreed with that of Madame de Tocqueville, that he would come in, and that he would do harm. He was admitted to be the second speaker in France, Guizot being the first.

'I have always opposed Guizot,' said Beaumont; 'I think him a bad politician and a bad judge of French feeling; but he is a grand speaker.'

'I have only known two men,' said Cousin, 'who were really ambitious; they were Lamartine and Guizot; the rest have been only vain. Lamartine, however, is both.'

In the evening I had an opportunity of talking separately to Molé, Beaumont, Tocqueville, and Cousin. I said to each of them, 'I think that it is probable that I shall be here again next May. Can you prophesy, or will you guess, what will then be the state of things? Shall I find the Government as it is now, consisting of an Executive Commission and an Assembly, or will there be two Chambers and a President, or no Chamber and a Dictator, or Louis XIX., or Henri V.?'

Not one would venture on even a conjecture. All that they agreed in was their expectation of another street fight within the next three months, and their belief that the Anarchical party, which they estimate at about 15,000, will be destroyed in it. The National Guards and the Army will show no mercy this time. The Anarchists have inflicted on them the Republic, ruined their trade, and wasted their time, and they are resolved to take the first opportunity of getting rid of them for ever.

It must be recollected, however, that this was the language held six weeks ago. Then, as now, we were told that the first opportunity would be seized, or one made, to crush the enemies of order. Such an opportunity occurred on the 15th. But no use was made of it. It occurred again when Sobrier and his 200 Montagnards defied the whole force of Paris. It occurred again when the Garde Républicaine, not amounting to 1,500 men, were allowed for several hours to refuse obedience to the Government, and to hold the Préfecture de Police against an army, and at length were bribed into submission.

A Frenchman is never bold when he is on the defensive. A few hundreds of the lowest street rabble, without arms or leaders, will attack an established Government, raise barricades under fire, and die content if they have enjoyed the excitement of bloodshed and riot. 200,000 men, armed and disciplined, seem paralysed if the law is on their side and they are required not to attack but to resist. Their cowardice when they are in the right, is as marvellous as their courage when they are in the wrong. Perhaps the reason is that in the former case they cannot rely on one another: in the latter case they can. Among the conservative ranks many may be lukewarm, and some, as was shown on the 15th, may be treacherous. They may only be making a show of resistance.

The Anarchists must be sincere. Whatever, however, be the explanation, it is certain that in Paris

Thrice is he armed that hath his quarrel wrong.

As for the Garde Mobile, everyone seems convinced that its days are numbered. Its creation was a wise measure. 15,000 of the outcasts of a great town, thieves, chiffonniers, and vagabonds, unable some to obtain employment for want of character, and others to keep it for want of self-control, the Lazzaroni of Paris, were turned at once, by giving them good pay, little to do, and above all by flattering their vanity, into the supporters of the Government. The love of excitement and of fighting, and the indifference to life which characterise the lowest classes in Paris, necessarily make them take part in every *émeute*. They will now fight *for* the National Guards ; left to themselves they would have fought *against* them. But as Gardes Mobiles, they are in fact soldiers: always under arms, and liable to be sent on any service ; but with double the pay of the regular army, and with the privilege of choosing their own officers. It is impossible that the regular army (La Ligne as I always hear it called) can long tolerate this comparison. A Pretorian body, selected from the best of the regular army, is an object of envy. Here we have a Pretorian body selected from the refuse of society. It cannot, however, be disbanded: such a measure would double the anarchical force. It will be sent therefore to some place in which it will be destroyed by the enemy or by the fatigues of the first campaign. Perhaps towards Italy to perish in a mountain campaign in the Alps. Perhaps to Algiers to melt away under a tropical sun.

In the meantime they make an amusing part of the armed population of Paris. They have been thrown together without classification, so you see marching side by side boys apparently of fifteen and men of fifty, tall rawboned ruffians and little scamps not half the height of their own muskets. They are said to have acquired tolerable habits of drill, but their general behaviour has very little that is military. At their posts they are sitting, lying down, and smoking, and their head-quarters in the Champs Elysées is a sort of fair. You see fifty of them in their uniforms filling the carriages of a merry-go-round or crowding before a puppet-show.

We talked of English statesmen, and Molé pronounced an eulogium on Lord Lansdowne—one of the wisest, the best-informed, and, above all, the least vain man that he had ever known. Next to him Lord Aberdeen was the favourite.

Friday, May 26.—I breakfasted with the Tocquevilles. We talked of Lamartine.

Tocqueville said ' that it was difficult to speculate as to his conduct, as he is an incoherent, inconsistent thinker and actor—that he feared that Lamartine looked on the present unsettled state of things as favourable to his pre-eminence ; that if he had thrown over Ledru Rollin and the Anarchists, which he might have done with perfect ease, in fact by merely remaining passive, he would certainly, for a time, have been at the head of the moderate party, though he would have had in it formidable rivals, but that among the Anarchists he is supreme. That it flatters his vanity to be worshipped by his own party, at least by the party now in power, and to be worshipped by the other party as the man who tempers and diminishes the mischievousness of his associates. Though in debt he is not corruptible by money. He does not receive company because he says, " Je n'ai pas le sou." '

Tocqueville asked him, why he did not require a salary from the Assembly. He answered, Because it might diminish his influence.

Tocqueville expressed a fear that the Republicans would try to economise by taking away the salaries of the priests. He would rather, if possible, increase them. They have considerable influence among the peasantry, and are indeed supposed to have affected materially the return of the present Assembly, and if they were better paid, a better class would enter the Church. He wishes too to alter their education, which is now carried on in seminaries admitting no others; so that they come into a world, of which they know nothing, to direct it.

I mentioned Guizot's remark to me, that in the Revolution of 1789 the 'Peuple' considered the high-born and the rich as personal enemies; abolished their titles, burnt their houses, confiscated and subdivided their estates, drove them into exile, put them to death, and tried, by enforcing equal partition among their descendants, to prevent the recurrence of large fortunes; but that in 1848 the 'Peuple' treated them not as enemies, but as slaves, not as a class to be hunted down, but to be kept in preserves, and consumed from time to time as the wants of the 'Peuple' required.

Tocqueville said that the remark was very just, and that he had himself perceived the gradual transition in the minds of the people, from dislike of the rich, to indifference, and ultimately to the sort of affection which one feels for one's milch cows, or one's poultry yard.

'During the Restoration,' he said, ' I was thought an aristocrat, and was unpopular in my department. After 1830 the people felt that they had beaten us down, and that there was little ground for any apprehension of our recovering our power. Still there was just enough fear of us to make them distant and cold. But this time, in 1848, all is changed. The people feel that as a political party, the gentry are extinct. They elected me by an immense majority; they would not injure any of my father's châteaux for all the world. They are quite ready to tax us, but they have no wish to plunder us, much less to do us any personal harm.'

He went on to say that one of the most striking changes which he had witnessed was the decrease of the influence of women. Formerly, every young artist, or poet, or preacher, or even politician, must come out chaperoned by some patroness. The ladies in the salons of the Faubourg St. Germain were the terror of Bonaparte. Under the Restoration they decided elections, influenced majorities in the Chamber, and were still more powerful at court. But now their influence is crushed by the magnitude of the events. No female hand has meddled with this revolution.

[Mr. Senior left Paris on the 27th.—ED.]

CORRESPONDENCE.

London, January 29, 1849.

My dear M. de Tocqueville,—I have begged Mr. Bancroft to take with him copies of two papers of mine in the last 'Edinburgh Review,' which, I think, may interest you and Madame de Tocqueville.

My time since I left you in Paris in May has been spent partly in Ireland, partly in the West of England, and partly, I am sorry to say, in my own room, under an attack of bronchitis, from which I recovered about three weeks ago. Yours has been more agreeably and more usefully employed. I was delighted, like the rest of the world, with your défence of property. Mrs. Grote thinks of making it a peg for an article on Pauperism.

We are to have Committees in each House on the Irish poor laws.

They will contain illustrations valuable to a political economist. Experiments are made in that country on so large a scale, and pushed to their extreme consequences with such a disregard to the sufferings which they inflict, that they give us results as precious as those of Majendie.

I am sorry that you have resigned the mission to Brussels, though I fear that the Congress may separate with little result. The pretensions of Austria and of Sardinia are separated by a gulf which diplomacy cannot fill.

I very much fear, from a very long conversation which I had yesterday with the Sardinian Minister, Marquis Sauli, that the people of Piedmont and Genoa will force their Governments into a fresh war with Austria. It seems that they think their honour requires them to make a second fight. I only hope that, if they are beaten, as I fear must be the case again, they will acquiesce in a second defeat.

I look forward with some anxiety to our parliamentary proceedings. A grave attack will be made on the Government as to both their Irish and their foreign policy. And I do not see how they can defend either. Their Irish poor-law extension, passed in 1846, was brought in against the better judgment of the wisest part of the Cabinet, in obedience to ignorant popular clamour—and has done, what was not easy, aggravated enormously both the moral and physical evils of that country. Their foreign policy appears to me to have been good, as far as France is concerned—but in Italy detestable. Their willingness to acknowledge the Duke of Genoa as King of Sicily was the most absurd and most wicked breach of the law of nations that has occurred in my time.

How Lord Palmerston will defend it I cannot conceive, and, if he falls, the Government can scarcely stand. I hear that he maintains that Metternich is still governing Austria from Brighton. If so, this is the most successful part of his long administration.

We regret the failure of Cavaignac very much—not the less, as it deprives us of M. de Beaumont, who was, as might have been expected, most popular here. Can you tell me anything of Admiral Cécile, his successor—nobody here seems to have heard his name?

Pray tell me your own news; and whether we may hope to see you and Madame de Tocqueville in the summer. Since I saw you we have added to our establishment a daughter-in-law, a very charming person. Still we have a couple of bedrooms vacant for our friends;

but if the daughter-in-law is followed by grandchildren, they will be turned into nurseries. So I hope that you will come to us while there is room. I hope myself to be in Paris in May. In August we shall probably be at Carlsbad, and in September and October in Italy, if the Liberals will let us.

Best regards to you and Madame de Tocqueville, from all our circle.

Ever yours,
N. W. SENIOR.

March 8, 1849.

My dear Mr. Senior,—You wrote to me the kindest and most interesting letter, and I reproach myself for not having answered it.

I am all the more guilty as my political duties are trifling, and I have not wanted time for correspondence. Perhaps this may be the cause of my laziness. The exhaustion which has succeeded to the feverish excitement of last year, renders me incapable of any effort, even the very agreeable one of writing to my friends.

This universal listlessness is the characteristic of the period.

On the one hand we have our present Assembly, decrepid, feeble, in whose discussions we do not care to take a part; and on the other the prospect of a new Chamber, the spirit of which is still enveloped in mystery, while its approach holds the whole political machine in suspense.

When I say that the spirit of the new Assembly is still a secret, I am not perfectly accurate.

The immense majority of the legislative body which will assemble next May will certainly be animated by a strong spirit of opposition and even of reaction to all the mad follies, all the false systems, and all the men who rose up in the early days of the revolution of February 1848.

But how far will it go in this direction?

Will it be sufficiently obedient to the violent instincts of the agricultural masses, whence it will have sprung, to go so far as to overthrow the Republic?

If it should go so far, what will it set up in the place of the Republic?

This is what is completely hidden behind the thick curtain of the Future. If I dared to raise it for a moment, I should say that the most probable course still appears to me to be the maintenance, at least provisionally, of the Republic.

The new Chamber will be composed of three or four parties, of which each would prefer the maintenance of the Republic to the triumph of its old enemies.

I think that these parties, having no hope of the success of their favourite project, will be forced to be satisfied with the government which is next best after the one which they would prefer.

This, at least, is what I catch a glimpse of in the midst of the darkness which surrounds us.

Our Constitution is very bad, but it may get better; and if material prosperity, which is beginning to revive, could be completely restored, the masses would before long become attached to the Republic, which is, one must own, well suited to our social condition, as well as to the passions and ideas to which that social condition has given rise.

So much for the future. As to the present, France exhibits at this moment the most extraordinary and to most people the most startling spectacle that could possibly be conceived.

Do you know what is the actual consequence of this ultra-democratic revolution, which has extended the suffrage beyond even the limits known in America? You would certainly find it difficult to guess.

The actual consequence of this revolution has been to give to the rich and even to the old nobility a political influence which they had lost for sixty years.

The men belonging to these classes are those whom the people everywhere select for election to offices of State.

There is another phenomenon: this revolution, which appeared destined to continue and perhaps to surpass the work of 1793, has restored not only to religion but to the clergy an influence a thousand times greater than the Restoration, which actually ruined itself for their sake, was able to do.

What say you to all this? Is it not a curious scene in the great drama of human affairs, and one well worth studying?

I think that I could easily disentangle and explain to you the causes, mostly accidental, which have quite naturally brought about this strange reaction, and why I think that it would be wrong to expect the results to be very durable, though they will be of great importance. But such a subject cannot be treated in a letter. It requires a long conversation.

Come and see us. The events passing in France deserve the attention of a clear and strong mind, such as yours.

Mr. Bancroft brought us the two pamphlets which you confided to him. Thank you warmly for them; they appear to be both interesting and instructive. How much I wish that I could go and thank you in person, and accept your kind and pressing invitation. It would be unfortunately impossible for us just now. But if I should not be elected, I will certainly take advantage of your friendly offer after the general elections. This chance, which universal suffrage renders always possible, does not, however, seem to me to be probable. I would rather therefore meet you here.

Remember me very particularly to Mrs. and Miss Senior, and believe me to be yours sincerely and affectionately,

A. DE TOCQUEVILLE.

Kensington, April 22, 1849.

My dear M. de Tocqueville,—A thousand thanks for your letter of March 8, which has given me more information and better views as to France than I have had since I left it.

I am thinking of being in Paris from about the 9th to

the 23rd of May, if I am likely to find you there; but I fear that you and my other friends will either be absent from Paris, canvassing, or, if in Paris, be so engaged as not to be visible. And in that case visiting Paris would be merely tantalising.

Pray tell me how things will be, then.

If you have looked at our debates you will have seen that our Government has not been very successful.

Their rate-in-aid for the distressed Irish Unions must be given up.

Lord Palmerston's foreign policy has been a series of blunders—except as respects you.

Peel has risen far above Lord John in public estimation. Nothing but his unwillingness to take office, and the weakness of each of the other two parties, Protectionists and Radicals, keep the present party in.

I hope that we shall get through our Irish difficulty by the only expedient—emigration. We sent 200,000 people from Ireland in 1847, and rather more in 1848. And I have no doubt that a still larger number will go this year.

The United States are quite ready to take 300,000 a year, and our own colonies 200,000. I never believed such an enormous emigration to be possible.

I trust that you will be a member of the next Assembly. If not, we rely on your and Madame de Tocqueville's promised visit. Best regards to you and to her from us.

Ever yours,
N. W. SENIOR.

May 9, 1849.

I cannot describe to you, my dear Mr. Senior, the annoyance I feel at the mischance which has befallen me.

I am obliged to leave Paris, and I shall not be able to be there during the few days of your visit.

My health has been so much shaken by the agitations and the labours of the last twelvemonth, that the doctors peremptorily order me to avoid Paris for some weeks, in order to take the rest and recreation which have become indispensable.

They declare that I shall be incapable of taking any part in the Chamber, in the very probable case of my election, unless it is preceded by this interval of complete relaxation. I yield to them with extreme regret. In the first place, I regret our not meeting; and in the second, that I shall not be present at the close of this Assembly and the opening of the next. But I must submit.

Ever yours,

A. DE TOCQUEVILLE.

[M. de Tocqueville's absence from Paris was a very great disappointment to Mr. Senior. There is therefore no mention of him in the next journal. To supply the omission Mrs. Grote has kindly furnished me with the following notes.—ED.]

In April 1849, Mr. Grote and I went to Paris, for the first time since the revolution of February 1848. Some of our friends gave us interesting particulars of the events which had passed in Paris, and of certain incidents which occurred to themselves, during the last twelve months. The interest which attached to the details of the terrible days of June 1848 surpassed all the rest. On the morning, I think, of the 24th, M. de Tocqueville (then a Député), left his house in the Rue Castellane, to repair to the Chamber. He had not proceeded far before he perceived signs of extensive agitation, and when he reached the Chamber of Deputies a strong conviction presented itself to his mind that some formidable conflict was at hand. The Chamber on that morning appointed a certain fraction of its members to attend officially in different quarters of the city where fighting was going forward. They were directed to tie their tricoloured scarves about their waists, and to animate and encourage by their presence the efforts made by the National Guards to suppress the revolutionary movement. M. de Tocqueville with two others (one of whom was M. Goudchaux, afterwards Minister of Finance) was ordered to the quarter in which the Louvre is situated. M. Goudchaux proved himself a stout-hearted citizen. He manfully seconded M. de Tocqueville in his endeavours to inspire the civic guard with courage and determination. There was, however, but little need of these endeavours; the National Guards were full of the best sentiments. When M. de Tocqueville would cry out, 'Now, my lads, press your advantage; another drive at them and the barricade is taken!' they would shout out, 'Ah! M. le Député, laissez-nous faire,—we know what we have got to do—Vive la République!' When M. de Tocqueville found his name drawn for the service I have here specified, he felt that he was 'in' for a struggle of the most momentous character. He had but just time to pen a hasty note to his wife, which ran thus: 'Leave Paris immediately, and do not return till you hear from me.' Madame de Tocqueville, guessing the gravity of the circumstances, also lost no time in obeying her husband's mandate. Taking all the money she had in the house, and concealing it upon her person, she repaired to St. Germain-en-Laye, and there awaited, in a state of mind of the most painful anxiety and suspense, such news as might arrive from the scene of action. She stayed there three nights (these were the dreadful days of June), during which she was without any authentic information concerning M. de Tocqueville. I think it was on the fourth day that, her uneasiness and impatience getting the better of her conjugal obedience, she ventured back to Paris. During her seclusion at St. Germain, she continually heard the lower class of people discussing on the events which were passing in Paris. The prevailing sentiment seemed to be a cordial desire that the insurgents should gain the victory, whilst a great number appeared disposed to go up to Paris and assist their brother 'Rouges.' This of course increased her already anxious sufferings.

M. de Tocqueville had returned home a few hours before her. He had scarcely had any repose during the whole of this fearful struggle. His domestic servant Eugène fought valiantly by his master's side, but both fortunately had come through unhurt. M. de Tocqueville described the condition of Paris during the second day of the conflict as being intensely agitating. The streets were deserted, except by combatants : all the 'portes-cochères' closed. At night you might hear a foot fall. Here and there a man would be seen lurking under a doorway, armed. Everyone suspected the presence of enemies in the upper windows, from whence musket-balls were frequently heard to whiz. On the second day M. de Tocqueville had serious misgivings as to the final result, but on the third morning he felt tolerably certain that the victory was passing to the side of the *bourgeoisie*. A day or two after the struggle had ceased, and the ' Rouges ' were beginning to hide their heads again, Madame de Tocqueville's cook came to her and said : 'Madame ought to know that the concierge of our house is a Rouge, and that he bears my master an ill grudge for his conduct during the fight.' Madame de Tocqueville asked how she knew this. ' I have it,' replied the cook, 'from our greengrocer, where he goes, and where he permits himself to use very threatening expressions in relation to M. de Tocqueville. He said yesterday, " Il y a longtemps que j'en veux à ce gredin-là."' Upon this, Madame de Tocqueville became extremely uneasy, and besought her husband to be upon his guard against the concierge. M. de Tocqueville (of whom his father once said to me, 'Alexis does not know what fear is') took little heed of his wife's warnings. But it happened that, very soon afterwards, he had occasion to stay out somewhat late, returning to his dwelling some time after the inmates of the hotel had retired to rest. He knocked at the 'porte-cochère;' and the concierge opened it in person. (It is customary in large hotels in Paris for the concierge to pull a string from his bed which unlatches the outer gate when anyone wishes to enter after a certain hour.) The concierge accosted him thus: 'Do you know, M. de Tocqueville, that I am very much alarmed at some unaccountable noises, which seem to proceed from a building at the farther end of our court?' Now this building was a disused stable or cowhouse, and was at some distance up a narrow garden court. 'Well, what do you want me to do?' said M. de Tocqueville. 'Oh,' replied the concierge, 'if Monsieur would be so good as to come with me; for I am afraid to go alone, and yet I should like to know from whence these odd noises proceed.' M. de Tocqueville instantly saw that this was a pretext to entice him to a lonesome spot. But he dissembled his suspicions, and told the concierge that he did not believe that there was any ground for alarm, but, as he wished it, he would go and assist him in his search. 'Allons,' cried he, 'we will soon find out the ghost. Do you march first, since you carry the light.' The concierge was a stout, square-built man, of middle height. M. de Tocqueville is a small man, but not destitute of muscular strength. At this particular period he habitually carried in his breast pocket a small, loaded pistol, and, as he followed the concierge up this long silent entry, he kept his right hand upon the weapon. When they got to the stable, the concierge made signs to him to listen attentively; they did so, but no sounds, except the sighing of the wind, were heard. After a few minutes, M. de Tocqueville, more than ever convinced that it was a feint for drawing him into an ambush, told the concierge that 'there was nothing, and that he must now light him back into the hotel.' They ascended the stairs to M. de Tocqueville's own door, of which he had the key. Turning to the concierge, he bade him 'good night!' in a firm voice, without any symptom of distrust. The man wished him 'good night!' in his turn, and went downstairs again. Not long afterwards M. de Tocqueville left this hotel, and took another apartment. They could not rid themselves of this very disagreeable functionary, who was the servant of the landlord of the hotel, and he chose to keep the concierge in the lodge.

Alexis de Tocqueville probably owed his escape from the designs of the 'Rouge' to his insisting on the latter preceding him. He never once suffered the concierge to get near to or behind him, and the latter probably guessed M. de Tocqueville to be 'ready for him,' by his keeping his hand in his bosom.

H. GROTE.

[Louis Bonaparte was President, M. Faucher was Prime Minister, and M. de Tocqueville was Minister for

Foreign Affairs when Mr. Senior next visited Paris, on his way to the Pyrenees, in July. There are no letters to be found on either side during this interval.—ED.]

CONVERSATIONS.

Paris, July 27, 1849.[1]—Mrs. Senior and I went at about twelve to Madame de Tocqueville, whom we found in the Hôtel des Affaires Étrangères, sitting with a large bag of five-franc pieces before her, and an *employé* in the Foreign-office, who is her secretary of charities, by her side making out a list of the people among whom the contents of the bag were to be distributed. The table was covered with begging-letters. I looked at two or three of them. One was from the widow of a *littérateur*, another from a tradesman ruined by the revolution. None of them were supported by any peculiar claims on the Foreign Minister. He was applied to merely as supposed to have a large income. Madame de Tocqueville says that of course she makes inquiries, but that they are necessarily superficial, and that she must be constantly deceived, and, at a great sacrifice of time and money, probably does more harm than good. A poor-law seems to be as much wanted for the relief of the rich as of the poor.

We talked of the chances of a prorogation. She said that, from the moment it had been suggested, an alarm had been spread of a *coup d'état* intended by the President. She admitted that many of those around him were urging him to seize monarchical power, and

[1] This passage was retained in the *Journals in France.*—ED.

that, if his character had not altered since 1840, he might be supposed accessible to such a temptation; but she thinks that he has now too much sense to make an attempt the temporary success of which is very doubtful and the permanent success impossible; and she is sure that none of his ministers would assist him. 'They believe us,' she said, 'to be ambitious conspirators; but all that we attempt, and all that we hope, is to keep our own heads and properties, and to protect those of our countrymen. We ourselves have removed nothing from our own house. We are birds of passage in this hotel.'

Saturday, July 29.—We dined with the Tocquevilles.

He hopes that the peace between Piedmont and Austria is by this time settled.

I said that I had heard that the principal difficulty was a demand by Piedmont that Austria should grant an amnesty to the Lombards who endeavoured to promote the union of Lombardy and Piedmont—a demand which appeared to me inadmissible. The Milanese rebelled against their sovereign—a sovereign deriving his title, not from conquest or treaty, but from a succession of centuries. The Piedmontese, though at peace with Austria, made common cause with the rebels, invaded Lombardy and annexed it to Piedmont. They have been defeated and driven back. Austria is in possession of Lombardy and even of a part of Piedmont. That the beaten Government should attempt to dictate to the conqueror the terms which he is to grant, not to them, but to his own subjects, is a pretension unparalleled in history.

Tocqueville did not object to this, but said that the

demands of Austria for the expenses of the war were at first excessive—far beyond the ability of Piedmont. He had reason to think, however, that they had been very considerably moderated, and this was the ground of his hope that the peace was arranged, if not signed.

We talked of Lord Palmerston's policy respecting Germany. He said that he thought it too favourable to Prussia.

I answered that, as Austria was in danger of falling to pieces, would be powerless if she lost Hungary, and under the influence of Russia if she kept it, it was important to raise up a substitute to stand between Western Europe and Russia, and that Prussia was the only Power capable of performing this office, and therefore that, if Lord Palmerston's policy tended to this, it was right. He replied that this might be true as respected the interests of England, but that France could not see with pleasure the farther aggrandisement of a great military Power immediately on her frontier.

Monday, July 30.—We called on Madame de Tocqueville, and found her as before with her bag of five-franc pieces and her almoner, deciding on petitions. She said that the rising on June 13 was far more serious than it was generally supposed to be. As the Hôtel des Affaires Étrangères is very much exposed, she removed all her papers and valuables to her own house, and the *économe*, or house-steward, contributed to the establishment by Bastide, entertained her with assurances of the triumph of the 'République Rouge.'[1]

[1] See Mrs. Grote's note, p. 63.—ED.

'I thought,' she said, 'after you left us yesterday, how much your conversation showed that you belonged to a settled government. You are to be absent for three months, and you have no doubt that when you return Queen Victoria will be still on her throne, and Lord John Russell still her Minister, and Mr. Senior still Master in Chancery. No Frenchman can look forward for three months, or, indeed, for three weeks.'

October 21, 1849.—We passed August and September in the Pyrenees, and returned to Paris in October.

In the evening I went to Madame de Tocqueville's.

I talked to Tocqueville about the late debate on the Roman question. Montalembert, he said, was splendid; nothing could be finer as a piece of oratory. La Rivière rather repeated an article than made a speech.

I asked Tocqueville whether he felt his habits as a writer interfere with his speaking. He said, Terribly. That ever since he had been in the Chamber he had been endeavouring in vain to shake off the writer. The only writer whom he recollected as having done this thoroughly was Guizot.

Tuesday, October 23.—I breakfasted with the Tocquevilles. Knight Bruce, who was of the party, asked Tocqueville if much attention was paid to the decree abolishing titles. He answered, that it was attended to in official acts, but neglected in society. I said that, even before it passed, titles had been in a great measure disused—for instance, that Tocqueville had never used his.

No, he said, though his father and his brother did;

but that he had always foreseen that some day titles would be abolished, and he did not wish to assume what he might have to relinquish.

I said that I was told that the distinction between *noble* and *roturier* existed in its full force in real life.

'Yes,' said Tocqueville, 'it does, meaning by noble, gentilhomme; and it is a great misfortune, as it keeps up distinctions and animosities of caste; but it is incurable—at least, it has not been cured, or perhaps much palliated, by our sixty years of revolution. It is a sort of Freemasonry. When I talk to a gentilhomme, though we have not two ideas in common, though all his opinions, wishes, and thoughts are opposed to mine, yet I feel at once that we belong to the same family, that we speak the same language, that we understand one another. I may like a bourgeois better, but he is a stranger.'

I mentioned the remark to me of a very sensible Prussian, *bürger* himself, that it was unwise to send out as ambassador any not noble. I said that it did not matter in England, where the distinction is unknown. 'Yes,' he replied, 'unknown with you; but you may be sure that when any of our *bürger* ministers meets one who is *von Adel*, he does not negotiate with him on equal terms; he is always wishing to sneak under the table.'

We talked of the physical exertion of public speaking. Knight Bruce said that after speaking for six hours, he felt tired for half an hour: Tocqueville, that he could not speak two days following, that he required an interval of rest for his throat, and that in the Chamber one was forced to scream, both to conquer the size of the room and the noise of interruptions.

I said that our reformed House was far more tolerant of bad speaking than the old House; that in the old House a bore was speedily coughed down; but that the anti-bore police was almost inefficient in the new House.

'With us,' said Tocqueville, ' it is not the bad but the good speakers that are unheard. In proportion as a speech tells, it provokes interruption: the bad ones are listened to, or at least submitted to, quietly enough.'

[Mr. Senior left Paris on the next day.—ED.]

CORRESPONDENCE.

[I have looked in vain for the original or a copy of the letter from M. de Tocqueville, to which the following is an answer. Large extracts from it are appended to the article on Lamartine published last year in the Journals in France and Italy, and to the Journal for 1849, vol. i. p. 214.—ED.]

Masters' Offices, December 10, 1849.

My dear M. de Tocqueville,—A thousand thanks for your interesting and instructive letter. I have ventured to add as notes to the article, of course not naming you, the two anecdotes of Lamartine. They confirm, I think, his account. When I was last in Paris I saw an enormous letter from Marshal Bugeaud, giving an account of what he saw and did on February 24. His story exactly tallies with Lamartine's. The story which you tell of the detachment of the 10th Legion, he tells thus: 'After the King's retreat I went home, changed my dress, and went back towards the Palais Bourbon. When I got there I met some deputies running out of the Chamber, frightened to death. Those who could speak cried, "All is over; they have proclaimed the Republic!" I ran to a detachment of the 10th Legion, which was stationed in the place, and said, "You don't wish for a Republic?" "No sacre bleu!" they said. "Then come with me to the Chamber." There were about 150 of them. They ran for their arms. Oudinot joined us, and we moved on the Chamber. About twenty deputies met us, escaping from the Chamber. "All is lost," they said; "the Duchess is going to the Invalides. The Republic is proclaimed." And it was too late, or we were too few, and so the monarchy fell. Had the Court been at Vincennes, had I had the command a fortnight sooner, things might have passed differently. But all had been neglected, no preparation made for resistance or for retreat, no plan laid down, no instructions given, no supplies of ammunition, no deposits of provisions, no collections of the tools necessary for breaking open doors and piercing walls; nothing was thought of except to follow what was recollected of the management of 1834. I have often talked to the ministers, and to M. Guizot, about the danger to which their want of preparation exposed the monarchy, but I never could excite their interest, or even gain their attention. There was a sort of sneer, as if they thought I was talking to get a command.'

Is not this your detachment of the 10th Legion?

What you say of the immediate causes of the Revolution is very important. *Mon siége est fait*—but this is not the last time that I shall write about the 24th of February.

I have no use for the proofs, unless perhaps you could send them to M. Pichot, the editor of the *Revue britannique*, with my compliments, and tell him that the article will come out in London in three weeks, and if he wishes to translate it for his review, and publish the translation at any time after that, they are at his service.

It is probable, however, that the Revolution has, among better things, destroyed the *Revue britannique*.

Lord Lansdowne was delighted with his French visit. He had an interview of some hours with your President, and negotiated a resumption of intercourse between him and Molé, who had ceased to visit the Élysée after the *coup d'état*. I have seen nobody else, being confined by bronchitis.

Kindest regards from all of us to you and Madame de Tocqueville. Ever yours,

N. W. SENIOR.

[There is a gap here in the correspondence. There is no letter on either side till after the next journal.—ED.]

CONVERSATIONS.

Paris, May 1850.—The law called afterwards 'The law of the 31st of May,' which restricted the suffrage, was at this time under discussion in the Assembly.

The foul copy of this journal was shown to M. de Tocqueville immediately after it had been written; and it was returned by him without alteration.

Some months afterwards I sent to him a fair copy, on which he made numerous notes, which are inserted after the conversations to which they refer.

Tuesday, May 14.—After breakfast I sat for half an hour with Tocqueville.

He utterly disapproves of what is going on, and, if he is to be ill, is glad to be ill now and to have nothing to do with it. His object, he says, has always been to make the best of the Constitution for the time being, and he believes that that which now exists might be made to work tolerably,[1] and this he thinks is the wish of *the majority*

---

[1] *Tuesday, May* 14.—Ceci demande quelques développements pour que ma pensée soit bien comprise.

Je doute très-fort qu'une constitution républicaine, ou, pour parler plus clairement encore, un pouvoir exécutif électif, convienne, quant à présent, à la France.

Je pense de plus, que la constitution républicaine de 1848 est extrêmement défectueuse, et j'ai prouvé que telle était mon opinion en votant contre plusieurs de ses principaux articles. Je crois qu'il est très-nécessaire qu'on arrive à la modifier, mais en même temps j'ai toujours été convaincu, et je le suis encore, que les périls qui naissent de l'exécution de la constitution, toute imparfaite qu'elle est, sont infiniment moindres que ceux qu'on ferait courir au pays en voulant briser cette constitution par la force, et en faisant

of the majority in the Assembly. They are not men of much experience, or of much knowledge, or, perhaps, of much talent—but they are honest. They have no leader, however. Odillon Barrot keeps retired, Dufaure is gone on some inquiry to Toulon; and the reactionary, or, as we now call them, the revolutionary party have it all their own way. They believe that the next Chamber must at all events be Montagnard. He does not know what rashness and folly on the part of the Government

prendre au parti modéré la responsabilité d'une révolution nouvelle. Je n'ai point de doute, comme je le disais dans la conversation ci-dessus rapportée, que cette manière de voir ne fût et ne soit encore partagée par ce que j'ai appelé *la majorité de la majorité* de l'Assemblée, c'est-à-dire, par cette masse d'hommes que les passions de parti, les calculs, ou les regrets de l'ambition, ou enfin la peur, ne conduisent pas. Il me serait facile de dire pourquoi les dangers qui naîtraient d'un renversement violent de la constitution seraient plus grands que ceux qui naissent de son maintien, mais je n'ai voulu ici qu'éclaircir les idées que j'ai déjà exprimées à M. Senior et non en produire de nouvelles.—*A. de Tocqueville.*

This passage requires development in order that my meaning may be perfectly understood. I much doubt whether a republican constitution, and, to speak still more plainly, an elective executive, is suitable to France in her present condition. I think, likewise, that the Republican Constitution of 1848 is extremely faulty, and I have proved that such is my opinion by voting against many of its principal articles. I believe that it is quite necessary to modify them, but at the same time I have always been convinced, and I am so still, that the dangers which arise from enforcing the constitution even in its present imperfect state would be infinitely less than those which the country would incur if it were to be overturned by violent means, and the responsibility of a new revolution laid upon the moderate party. As I said in the above conversation, I have no doubt but that this opinion was and is shared by *the majority of the majority* in the Assembly; that is to say, by all those who are moved neither by party spirit, by interest, by ambition, nor by fear. It would be easy for me to show how it is that the perils occasioned by a violent overthrow of the constitution would be greater than those which arise from its maintenance; but I wished here only to clear up the ideas which I have already expressed, not to add new ones.

may do; but he is sure that, with tolerable prudence, it would not be so. These recent Parisian elections are mere protests against counter-revolution. The people see that the Government is conspiring against the Republic, and try to warn it.

I mentioned Z.'s parallel of the present state of things to that which preceded the election of the Convention.

'I wish,' answered Tocqueville, 'that all our history could be burnt, if this is the use that is made of it. The next Assembly will be no Convention unless they make it one. No one is deceived by the protests of the reactionary, or, as they call themselves, the Conservative party. No one believes that they really care about improving the constituencies. Their real objects are two. One is to engage the whole majority of the Assembly in a counter-revolutionary course, to bring them gradually, by a series of measures each a little more unconstitutional than the previous one, into an anti-republican position. The other is to produce a revolt, a victory, and an anti-republican Constitution, probably a presidency for ten years, surrounded by monarchical institutions. In the first attempt they probably will succeed. The really moderate portion of the Assembly will find itself counter-revolutionary before it is aware of what it has done. In the latter they will probably fail. The adverse chances are too many. In the first place an *émeute* is improbable. The leaders of the Montagne are perfectly satisfied with their position. The twenty-five francs a day, though they are obliged to surrender much of it to the public purse of the party, is still a great deal to men who had nothing before they were deputies, and will have nothing after they cease to be so. They are afraid too of their followers—they know that they will themselves be the first victims of a "rouge" republic. They will strive to prevent a revolt, and I think will prevent one. In the second place, if there be a fight, the *émeutiers* may succeed. The reactionists are very confident, but I have seen too many confident parties beaten to be sanguine. The 10,000 *graciés* have nothing to lose. They have a fair pretext to fight for. If the Government was unpopular before it brought in this law,[1] what will it be afterwards? I hope that the National Guard will be stanch; but 125,000 of its members voted for Sue. Many thousands of them will be among the disenfranchised. If they side with the *émeute*, the soldiers can no longer be relied on. Thirdly, suppose the battle fought and won. I am not sure that the majority of the present Assembly would vote an anti-republican constitution. They might the day after the victory, but I doubt whether they would three weeks after. And what sort of an anti-republican constitution would work? I foresee no prospect of alteration in our present situation, unless accident should offer one; and as for its ending, that seems as far off as it was in 1789.'[2]

[1] The law, then under discussion, passed on May 31, 1850, restricting the suffrage.—ED.

[2] Ceci demande encore un développement pour être bien compris.

J'entends par 'the ending of the present situation' un état stable et définitif, devenant la manière d'exister pour la société pendant un long

Thursday, May 16.—I drank tea with the Tocquevilles. As he does not admit the usual explanation that the whole matter was a scheme to insult France, he is as much puzzled by the Greek affair as I am. His intercourse with Lord Palmerston led him to believe him faithful to his engagements, though troublesome, litigious, and unscrupulous. He has the *esprit d'un procureur* (which was also Beaumont's expression), but also of an honest attorney—so far, at least, as an attorney can be honest![1]

espace de temps ; comme la monarchie administrative et sans contrôle politique qui a suivi chez nous les guerres civiles des 16me et 17me siècles, ou la monarchie représentative qui a achevé de se fonder en Angleterre après les révolutions de 1640 et de 1688. Je ne parle point d'un établissement transitoire qui impose momentanément la paix aux partis, laisse respirer la nation et lui permette de se jeter de nouveau avec ardeur à la recherche du bien-être matériel par des voies irrégulières.

Une solution de cette espèce ne peut pas beaucoup tarder, mais c'est de la solution dont j'ai d'abord parlé, que nous sommes encore, à mon avis, très-loin.—*A. de Tocqueville.*

This again demands some explanation to be perfectly understood. By the ' ending of the present situation,' I mean a stable, definitive condition, into which society might settle for a considerable period, such as the administrative and unfettered monarchy which followed with us the civil wars of the sixteenth and seventeenth centuries, or the representative monarchy which was ultimately founded in England after the revolutions of 1640 and of 1688. I am not speaking of a transitory government which imposes only a temporary peace on the different parties, and, after a breathing time, leaves the nation to plunge itself once more with eagerness into schemes for acquiring wealth by irregular means.

Such a solution as this cannot be long in coming, but the solution which I first mentioned is, in my opinion, still very distant.

[1] Lord Palmerston est un homme d'État de premier ordre, dont la politique appelle quelquefois à son aide les petites ruses et les expédients d'un 'attorney.'—*A. de Tocqueville.*

Lord Palmerston is a statesman of the first class, whose policy sometimes calls to its assistance the cunning and petty expedients of an attorney.

I asked in what respect unscrupulous.

'He seemed to me,' answered Tocqueville, 'to interfere in the affairs of the Continent for the purpose of serving his own personal or party interest at home, with little regard to the consequences on the rest of Europe. He ought to have known in 1847 that he could not stir the inflammable elements of Rome and Naples without risking a general conflagration.'

'The conflagration,' I answered, 'was caused by your revolution, and who in 1847 foresaw that? I remember your saying to me in October in that year that Louis Philippe was the most autocratic sovereign that had reigned over France since Charlemagne—that he approached nearer to absolute power than Louis XIV.'

'Yes,' replied Tocqueville, 'he *was* nearly absolute; but it was of the extent, not of the durability, of his power that I spoke. He had so thoroughly corrupted the Chamber that he had no parliamentary opposition to fear. He had so thoroughly corrupted the 200,000 electors that he had nothing to fear from an electoral opposition. With his 200,000 or rather 400,000 places, all the middle classes, on whom his government rested, were his tools. But, by abusing for these purposes the gigantic means conferred by our system of centralisation, he had rendered those middle classes, on whom his throne was built, unfit to sustain its weight. His monarchy was constructed with great skill and great solidity, but its foundation was a quicksand. He made the middle classes objects of hatred and contempt, and the people trampled them and him under foot. I never thought him during the latter years of his reign safe from a revolution.'

'No,' said Madame de Tocqueville, 'you prophesied one three years before it occurred.'

'Well,' said Tocqueville, 'this is what Lord Palmerston must have perceived. He must have known that all the Continent was mined. And he had no right to presume on his insular position and throw combustibles over the rest of the world.'

I asked how he liked Lord Normanby.

'Very much indeed,' he said. 'It was impossible for a minister to cultivate more anxiously a good understanding between the two countries. He pushed his endeavours to consult the feelings of France to the utmost extent that his duty to England would allow. Lately, however, he has excited much jealousy by his intimacy with Mrs. Howard. I once,' continued Tocqueville, 'encountered her at St. Cloud. I went there unexpectedly, and was introduced into the room where she was dining with a party of men. Lord Normanby frequents these parties. That perhaps is unavoidable; but he also visits her familiarly in her own house. He has the *grandes* and the *petites entrées* there.[1] Of course the motive is a wish to influence the President through her, and this we do not like. Lady Normanby delights everybody.'

We talked of a retreat for the winter. 'Hyères,' said Tocqueville, 'is charming. You live among groves

---

[1] I afterwards ascertained that M. de Tocqueville was quite misinformed. —N. W. S.

of oranges and lemons, with a fine sea and a pretty country; and you are safe, or nearly safe, from the scourge of the northern coast of the Mediterranean—the Mistral.'

'My delight,' said Madame de Tocqueville, 'is Algiers. The sky, the light, the mountains, and the sea are like nothing in Europe. Our sun is pale, our air is fog, our sea is muddy compared to those of Africa. But I cannot promise you comfort there. Your food will be good, but, whatever pains you take, your bed will be alive.'[1]

'On the whole,' said Tocqueville, 'my choice is Palermo. You have there a fine town, a delightful climate and country, plenty of society, and all Sicily for excursions.'

He left the room for a minute, and Madame de Tocqueville said, 'I don't tease him now about passing the winter out of France, but I think that he must do it. He cannot bear to quit the Assembly in such times as these; but, if he is not to speak, if he is not to write, if he is not to read or even to think about politics—and such are the orders of his physician—what is the use of his staying here?'

'Well,' he said when he came back, 'you have seen Madame de Cirourt. Did you remember that I begged you to let her know *que je lui trouve infiniment de l'esprit*. I see that you did not. You were anxious to promote your own interests in that quarter, and forgot mine. Pray remember it next time.'

[1] My experience was the reverse. The bed was good, the food was bad.—N. W. S.

He soon came back to politics. 'With the exception of the Montagnards,[1] and of a few really moderate members of the Opposition, everybody is conspiring against everybody. The Legitimists, the Orleanists, and the Bonapartists, are each furious against the two others, and all three are determined to overthrow the Republic. "Ils veulent en finir," they say, "avec ces gens-là." " En finir!" as if it were possible to kill, imprison, transport, or in any way to drive out of Paris 100,000 men. There will be no *fin* in our time, or in the time of our children. It must be confessed, however, that this revolutionary regimen does not suit us ill.[2] Every interval of convulsion has been succeeded by one of

[1] Il y a certainement là une nuance de ma pensée qui a échappé à M. Senior.
Il est impossible que j'ai dit que les Montagnards ne conspiraient pas. Ils ne conspirent pas pour détruire la forme républicaine, comme les trois autres partis nommés ensuite, mais ils conspirent assurément pour faire servir la République à une révolution sociale.—*A. de Tocqueville.*
Mr. Senior has not seized the exact shade of my idea. I cannot have said that the Montagnards were not conspiring. They are not conspiring, in order to overturn the Republic, like the three parties afterwards mentioned, but they certainly are conspiring to effect a social revolution by means of the Republic.

[2] Tout ce qui suit, jusqu'à la fin de la page, me paraît plus approbatif que ce que j'ai dû dire, et fondé sur des raisons non pas contraires à celles qui motivent mon opinion, mais un peu différentes.
L'expérience, en effet, nous a appris que chaque révolution change beaucoup de positions, développe beaucoup de besoins, fait naître beaucoup de désirs, répand un grand mouvement et une grande activité dans toutes les intelligences.
Quand le calme renaît dans le monde politique momentanément, toute cette agitation ne cesse pas entièrement, elle change seulement d'objet ; elle passe dans le monde industriel et commercial, et y fait faire des efforts plus grands et des tentatives plus hardies que si on était toujours resté dans une société calme.—*A. de Tocqueville.*
All that follows, to the end of the page, seems to me to express more

increased prosperity. Old prejudices are weakened, the experience of years is gained in months, and the most acute intellects and the most decided wills assume power. This revolution, however, has as yet been an 'exception. It has brought forward nobody except some *militaires*, and they came from Algiers. They are nearly the sole produce of that soil. We sow soldiers there broadcast, and we reap from time to time a general.'

Saturday, May 18.—After Gioberti left us I went to Tocqueville's. He is as puzzled as ever by the Greek affair,[1] but warns me not to believe the Government papers. The moderate party are resolved to turn out Lord Palmerston, and, if possible, the Whigs. No ministry that we could have in England would be Tory enough for them; but they think they could get a neutral one—one that, if it gave them no assistance, would, at least, interpose no obstacle to their restoring in Europe what they call order; that is, destroying every

approbation than I intended, and to be founded on reasons which are not contrary to those which influenced me, but different from them.

Experience, indeed, teaches us that every revolution changes many positions, developes many wants, rouses many desires, and excites great animation and activity in every mind. When calm is once more restored to the political world, all this agitation does not at once cease—but its object changes; it passes into the industrial and commercial world, and induces greater efforts and bolder schemes than would have been the case had the tranquillity of society remained undisturbed.

[1] The dispute with Greece arose out of demands made by our Foreign Minister for damages for certain injuries to British subjects (Mr. Finlay and Don Pacificos). These demands not being satisfied, Admiral Parker proceeded to blockade the Piræus. A misunderstanding with the French Government ensued which led to the recall of M. Drouyn de l'Huys fro m the Court of St. James'.—ED.

advance to liberality that has been made since 1830. For this purpose they are using every effort *pour envenimer la dispute*, and Lord Palmerston has most unfortunately assisted by putting them at present in the right. He himself would deeply regret their success, as respects the Whigs—always excepting Lord Palmerston, whom he is as anxious to get rid of as Berryer or De Broglie can be, since he believes the tranquillity of Europe incompatible with his presence in our Foreign Office.

I said that I had heard that something like this was supposed to have occurred in Switzerland—that Lord Palmerston had been accused of carrying on a double negotiation, and, while supporting the Sonderbund in London, of urging at Berne the revolutionary party to invade Lucerne.

He answered that he found in the French Foreign Office a tradition that such had been the case, though he had not examined the documents.

I mentioned the Abbé Gioberti's visit, and Tocqueville spoke of him with great pleasure. He had enjoyed a most agreeable breakfast with him and Cousin. This led us to talk of the general state of the Catholic clergy. I said that, with the exception of one or two Italians, I had never met in society a foreign priest; that at Gäesbeck in Belgium, Madame Arconati spoke to me in high terms of their priest, and that I asked if she could let me meet him at dinner; but she answered that he could not dine with the family; it would be uncomfortable for both parties.

Tocqueville replied that such was not the case in France; that in many *cures*, though of course comparatively few, the priest was a gentleman by birth; that if a son of his chose to take orders he should make no objection. In general, however, the priest is the son of a rich peasant; he is not a polished man, but he has manners that do not offend, and considerable information.[1] His worst fault is his pride. His morals are always pure. A dissolute priest would be hunted out of the country—but, whatever his personality, his profession entitles him to be treated as an equal. 'When you come to Tocqueville,' he added, 'you will find the curé dining frequently with me, and once a year Madame de Tocqueville and I dine with him. A brother of the predecessor of the present curé was my servant; the

---

[1] Le fait serait exagéré si on le présentait d'une manière si générale. Ce que M. Senior me fait dire est vrai, mais dépend des provinces. Dans tout l'ouest que je connais, et je crois, dans tout le midi, que je ne connais pas, le prêtre appartient (non pas peut-être en général, mais très-souvent) à des familles riches, ou du moins très-aisées. Dans les environs de Paris, par exemple, c'est le contraire. En général, partout où la foi a gardé de profondes racines, et où le prêtre reste très-honoré, à cause de son caractère saint, par la population, on remarque que le clergé se recrute dans des classes plus élevées que dans les provinces où la foi est pour ainsi dire éteinte, et où le clergé n'a pas d'influence sur les habitants.—*A. de Tocqueville.*

This statement would be an exaggeration if asserted without qualification. The remark which Mr. Senior quotes as mine is true, but applies only to certain provinces. In the west, with which I am personally acquainted, and, from what I hear, also in the south, the priest belongs (not, perhaps, in general, but very often) to a rich family, or at least to one in easy circumstances. In the neighbourhood of Paris, however, the contrary is the case. Generally speaking, wherever religion is deeply rooted, and the priest is venerated by the people on account of his sacred office, one sees the clergy recruited from a higher class than in those provinces where faith is extinct, and the clergy have lost their influence.

curé has dined with me while his brother waited, and neither of them perceived in this the least *inconvenance*.

'The institution is certainly a democratic one.[1] It places the peasant on a level with the noble, but the politics of the clergy are essentially conservative. They are dependent on the State for their salaries, and therefore cannot resist the party that is dominant for the time being, be it despotic or anarchical, but the tendency of their wishes and their habits is monarchical.'[2]

---

[1] Je ne crois pas avoir été aussi affirmatif. Je dois avoir dit, parce que je le pense, qu'il y avait dans la constitution du clergé catholique deux aspects, ou deux caractères qui permettaient à ce clergé de s'identifier assez aisément, soit à des institutions politiques aristocratiques, soit à des institutions politiques démocratiques. Par sa hiérarchie officielle de servants, curés, évêques, archevêques, pape, et sa subordination exacte, il tend vers l'aristocratie et la monarchie. Par le principe de son recrutement et de son avancement, qui repose uniquement sur la capacité et l'unit par les liens de l'origine à toutes les classes de la société, les plus basses comme les plus hautes, par sa doctrine, qu'aux yeux de l'église et de la religion tout au dehors du clergé doit être considéré comme égal et traité de même, le paysan comme le noble, il incline vers la démocratie.—*A. de Tocqueville*.

I do not think that I spoke so decidedly. I must have said, because I believe it, that the Catholic Church is so constituted as to have two aspects, or rather that it is composed of two different elements which enable the clergy to identify themselves easily enough either with aristocratical or democratical institutions. Its official hierarchy—its acolytes, priests, bishops, archbishops, and pope—and its rigid discipline are in their nature monarchical and aristocratical. The mode in which it is recruited, and its promotion, which rests entirely upon merit, bind it to every class of society, the highest as well as the lowest; and the principle which it holds, that in the eyes of the Church all are equal, apart from the clergy themselves, and should all be treated alike, peasant as well as noble, inclines it to democracy.

[2] Tout cela est très-vrai, mais il faut ajouter qu'au fond le clergé n'appartient qu'à lui-même, que les formes politiques seront toujours pour lui des choses secondaires; que les pouvoirs politiques qui ont cru l'avoir lié à leur fortune n'ont jamais manqué de se tromper, et qu'à ses yeux les affaires

I asked whether the regular clergy multiplied. 'Not,' answered Tocqueville, 'the mendicant orders: we have none of them now, nor of the comfortable orders, such as the Benedictines; but the number of the active orders—those engaged in education and charity—and also of the most austere, contemplative orders, such as the Trappists, augment strikingly. The Trappists are admirable cultivators. Their time, when not devoted to prayer, is spent in the fields. They are under excellent direction, work harder than our peasants, and are the great introducers of new instruments and processes. Those who have settled in Africa have magnificent herds and flocks. If you could tempt them in numbers into Ireland they would be the best improvers.'

May 19.—I dined with M. Anisson Duperron. The Duc de Broglie, M. de Viel Castel, and Baron de Billing were of the party. The Duke seemed much out of spirits. I drank tea with the Tocquevilles. I mentioned the depression of the Duc de Broglie.[1]

' He is one,'[2] said Tocqueville, ' of a numerous class

de l'église restent toujours les grandes affaires auxquelles tout le reste doit être subordonné.—*A. de Tocqueville.*

All this is very true, but it must be added that the clergy in truth owes allegiance only to the Church; that politics will never be of more than secondary interest for them; that the Governments which have fancied that they had bound them to their fortunes have never failed to be deceived; and that in their eyes the affairs of the Church will always be considered as the only important ones, to which all others should be subordinated.

[1] The father of the present ambassador.—ED.

[2] La phrase est construite de manière à faire croire que je place le duc de Broglie parmi ceux qui ont passé leur vie à croire que tout était fini : il y a une nuance qui a échappé à M. Senior, et ma pensée devrait être rédigée à peu près ainsi :—

' Le duc de Broglie est un de ces théoriciens politiques qui ont voulu

who at each successive phase of our Revolution have believed that it was over, and that a settled state of things was to ensue. My father is 76; he was about 16 at the time when the Revolution began. He recollects therefore the opinions that have prevailed during its progress. When fifteen years of disorder ended in a military despotism, everybody believed that it had run its course. It seemed to be the natural progress of events that revolution should produce war, and that war should make the army, and that the army should make its General omnipotent. When the Consulate and the Empire were followed by the Restoration, it seemed also in the order of things that the military ruler should be ruined by the ambition to which he owed his empire; that he should go on playing double or quits till he

prouver aux autres, et étaient parvenus à se prouver à eux-mêmes, que la Royauté de juillet était la fin naturelle de la révolution française, et commençait la nouvelle ère de la Société parmi nous. À chacune des différentes phases de notre révolution on a vu des hommes d'esprit tomber dans une erreur semblable.

'Nous avons le goût de la métaphysique politique, de quelques faits qui se ressemblent nous tirons volontiers de prétendues règles générales, dont nous nous servons ensuite pour expliquer tout ce qui a été, et prévoir tout ce qui sera.' Mon père, etc., etc.

This passage is worded so as to make it appear that I class the Duc de Broglie among those who have spent their lives in believing in finality. A shade of my meaning has escaped Mr. Senior, and my idea ought to be expressed pretty nearly in these terms:—

'The Duc de Broglie is one of those political theorists who wish to persuade others, and have succeeded in convincing themselves, that the Monarchy of July [1830] was the natural end of the French Revolution, and the commencement of a new era. At every new phase of our Revolution, men of ability have been seen to fall into a similar error.

'We have a taste for metaphysical politics: from some facts which resemble each other we like to draw some imaginary general rules, which we use to explain all that has gone before, and to foresee all that is to follow.'

had exhausted his good fortune; that his domestic enemies should join with his foreign ones; that the ancient dynasty should be restored, and that constitutional Royalty should become the permanent form of French government. When Charles X. tossed his crown into the hands of his cousin in 1830, this too seemed a natural conclusion of the drama. The parallel between France and England was now complete. In a restoration, it was said, the first king that is restored is so delighted with his return to power that he is willing to accept it on any terms.. And those terms he is likely to keep tolerably. He is determined not to have to travel again. The successor of the restored sovereign takes the crown not as a good fortune, but as a right. He feels the limits within which he is confined irksome, and easily believes them to be mischievous. His flatterers tell him that they are void; that his rights are unalienable, perhaps divine, and that it is his duty to save his country without looking nicely to the technical legality of the means which must be employed. He attempts to act on these principles, and is resisted and deposed. But a great ancient nation that has once tried the experiment of democracy will not repeat it. It will select for its new sovereign the next in succession who is willing and fit to accept the responsibility and submit to the restrictions of a constitutional monarch. In that dynasty the conflicting principles of legitimacy and selection, of divine right and popular right, are united. It may expect indefinite duration. Such a dynasty is in the second century of its reign

Every Form of Government transitory.

in England, and in the first century of its reign in France.

'The revolution of 1848 came, and these illusions were dissipated in an hour. The great monarchical fortress which was built for ages, proved to be a mere stage decoration. The Republic re-appeared with its single Assembly, its universal suffrage, its clubs, its journals, its forced paper currency. The line along which they have been travelling since 1830 turns out to have been only the segment of a circle. They believe that 1848 has brought them back to the point at which their fathers started in 1789. They fancy themselves now in 1791, armed without doubt with far more power and far more experience than were possessed by the Legislative Assembly, but also attacked by much stronger and much more practised enemies. I do not wonder at their despondency; indeed, I share it. The difference is that what seems strange to them seems natural to me. I have long seen that the Orleans family were mere actors, whose exit was approaching, and I fear that mere actors have followed them.'[1]

[1] Pour rendre plus complètement et plus exactement ma pensée, il faudrait ajouter :—

'Les hommes qui, comme le duc de Broglie, ont cru fermement la révolution finie, se livrent au désespoir, et joignent au mal réel dont nous souffrons mille maladies plus terribles encore, que leur esprit dérouté et leur imagination effrayée leur fait inventer. Moi qui suis convaincu depuis longtemps que le *sol social* de la France ne peut, quant à présent, donner d'assiette solide et permanente à aucun gouvernement, j'éprouve ces tristesses, mais non point ce profond découragement ni ces terreurs ; je ne crois pas que tout soit fini; je ne crois pas, non plus, que tout soit perdu, et je regarde mon pays comme un malade, qu'on ne peut, il est vrai, espérer aujourd'hui guérir, mais qu'on peut soulager beaucoup, dont on peut

We talked of La Hitte's despatch. He must have written it, Tocqueville thinks, himself, which a foreign minister, especially an inexperienced one like La Hitte, ought never to do. He should give full instructions as to the substance, but leave the form to those who have been bred up to the office, and know how to use the double-edged weapons of diplomatic controversy.

Madame de Tocqueville asked me if I had kept a journal. I said Yes, and that, if she wished to see it, I would send it to her the next morning. And I did so, ending with this page.

May 21.—I drank tea with the Tocquevilles, but saw little of him. It was the first day of the debate on the electoral bill, and one member after another came in and held a council with him in the next room. His longest conference was with Lamoricière. He came out of it rather exhausted. Lamoricière had thrown away his cigar only at the top of the stairs, and Tocqueville,

---

rendre pour le moment l'existence très-prospère, et de la maladie même duquel on peut faire sortir de grandes choses pour l'humanité et pour lui-même.—*A. de Tocqueville.*

To express my idea more completely and accurately, I should add: ' Those who, like the Duc de Broglie, have firmly believed the Revolution to be finished, give themselves up to despair, and join to the evil from which we are already suffering a thousand others still more terrible, the fruits of their disordered minds and terrified imaginations. As for me, who have long been convinced that the *social soil* of France cannot at present offer a solid and permanent foundation to any government, I suffer from the same depression, but not from the same terrors and despair : I do not believe that all is over, nor, on the other hand, that all is lost. I consider my country as a sick man whom we cannot, it is true, hope to cure at once, but whose malady one may greatly alleviate, whose existence may be rendered extremely prosperous, and whose very sufferings may be productive of great results, both for himself and for the whole human race.'

never very tolerant of tobacco, is peculiarly sensitive after his long illness. He said that he was *empesté*.

Madame de Tocqueville spoke highly of the wit and conversational powers of Lamoricière.

She amused me with an account of the schemes of some of the President's friends, I suspect of the lady members of the party. When the *émeute* takes place (for they have decided that there shall be one) the President is to show himself in the moment of triumph and march as Emperor to the Tuileries. Changarnier, of course, will be his competitor, but they rely on his beating him, as he is a better rider, and has the best horse in Paris.

La Hitte's letter recalling Drouyn de l'Huys, was not inserted in the body of the 'Moniteur.' It appeared in a supplement. Dupin, who, as president, transmits to the 'Moniteur' the official documents that are communicated to the Assembly, explained from his chair at some length the circumstances through which this happened. I forget what they were, but they proved that it was a mere accident.

The President (Louis Napoleon I mean), of his own authority, forbad the insertion of the letter. Hereupon La Hitte tendered his resignation, and, as a compromise, it was inserted in the supplement. I do not think that, in England, a Speaker of the House of Commons could be prevailed on to tell a series of deliberate falsehoods in order to conceal a Cabinet dispute.

May 22.—I drank tea with Tocqueville. Madame de Tocqueville was confined to her bedroom. Tocqueville returned to me my journal. He had read all that related to himself, and saw nothing to explain or to alter.[1]

'The great misfortune,' he said, 'of France is the preference of *égalité* to liberty.' I begged him to give me a lecture upon *égalité*—a term about which I had heard a great deal, without accurately comprehending its meaning.

'Generally,' he said,[2] 'it is a wish that no one should be

[1] The reader has seen, by the notes, that when M. de Tocqueville read the fair copy, some months later, he found much to alter.—N. W. S.

[2] Je ne saurais voir dans ce qui suit l'expression complète et nuancée de ma pensée. Je crois, cependant, mes paroles fidèlement reproduites, mais ce sont de ces paroles qu'on jette dans une conversation avec un ami, sans y attacher grande importance, et sans avoir la prétention d'approfondir le sujet dont on parle, se livrant plutôt à la disposition du moment qu'à une recherche sérieuse. Pour bien peindre ce qu'on doit entendre par la passion de l'égalité en France il faudrait une étude beaucoup plus détaillée des différents sentiments et des différentes idées dont cette passion s'alimente. Le portrait que j'en fais ici est vrai dans les parties qu'il représente, mais fort inexacte si l'on considère l'ensemble des traits de l'original.

Ce que je dis à la fin, que personne ne s'occupe de liberté, de garanties, et de bon gouvernement est de même vrai, mais d'une vérité restreinte : c'est une boutade de mauvaise humeur, plutôt qu'un jugement sérieux.— A. de Tocqueville.

I cannot admit that what follows expresses the exact shade of my meaning. I believe my words to be faithfully reported, but they are the sort of expressions which one utters at random in friendly conversation, without attaching much importance to them, and without any pretension to deal profoundly with the subject, following the whim of the moment rather than attempting a serious disquisition. To describe accurately what is meant by the passion for equality in France would require a much more detailed investigation of the different sentiments and ideas which feed this passion. The portrait drawn by me in this page is true in its separate features, but very inexact if compared with the general aspect of the original.

What I say in the end, that no one cares about liberty, security, or good government, is also true, but in a limited sense : it is rather an outbreak of ill-humour than a serious assertion.

better off than oneself; but, to explain it, I must begin historically. The *ancien régime* was the reign of privilege. All power, all distinction, and, as far as it was possible, all pleasure, was reserved for one caste. The people paid the taxes, the *noblesse* spent them. The people furnished the soldiers, the *noblesse* the officers; the people had nothing to do with the laws but to obey them; the *noblesse* made them and administered them. The *noblesse* alone were good company; if a *roturier* penetrated into their *salons* it was through their condescension.

'The Revolution destroyed this system, at least that part of it which, consisting in positive institutions, was destructible; but it could not destroy the social distinctions which depend upon manners. It could not enable the *bourgeois* to feel himself the equal of the *gentilhomme*. It could not deprive the noble of his superior manners, of his self-confidence, of the respect paid to his birth, or of many other advantages incident to his position. These things excite the envy of the *bourgeois*. Again, wealth, though less powerful with us than with you, gives great power. The rich man's son is better educated, and better launched, and better assisted. He gets on better, and this excites the envy of the poor. The great majority of the French consist, of course, of the low-born and the poor, and the *égalité* which they fight for is the destruction of the advantages of birth and wealth.

'This is the reason why they clamour against the use of substitutes in the army. Nothing would so much destroy the happiness of the higher orders as the forcing every young man, whatever were his birth or his fortune or his profession, to serve for three years as a private soldier. This is the reason why they cling to the law which limits testamentary power; why they will not tolerate a peerage, or an upper house, or a qualification. Socialism and Communism are the same feelings logically carried out. *Égalité* is an expression of envy. It means, in the real heart of every Republican, "No one shall be better off than I am;" and while this is preferred to good government, good government is impossible. In fact, no party desires good government. The first object of the reactionary party is to keep down the Republicans; the second, if it be the second object of each branch of that party, is to keep down the two others. The object of the Republicans is, as they admit, *égalité*—but as for liberty, or security, or education, or the other ends of government, no one cares for them.

(End of Journal of May 1850.)

Masters' Offices, Chancery Lane, London, July 17, 1850.

My dear M. de Tocqueville,—Mrs. Grote has just shown me your letter of June 25. I was delighted to think, as I read it, that you and Madame de Tocqueville must be really convalescent, for it does not read like a letter from a sick-house.

Friday, August 9, sets us, the slaves of the seal, free.

Pray tell me whether your kind plan that I should pass a few days with you, holds.

And if it perfectly suits you and Madame de Tocqueville's health and convenience to receive me, when shall I come?

M. Anisson Duperron has proposed to me to visit him at St. Antin. If I go to you, I can go to him either before or after.

We are all looking on with amazement at the doings of your Assembly. The monarchs of Europe need not fear the liberality of a republic.

I am inclined to think that civil liberty flourishes best under the protection of a throne, and religious liberty under that of a mitre.

With our united best regards to you and to Madame de Tocqueville, believe me, ever yours truly,

NASSAU W. SENIOR.

NORMANDY.

CHÂTEAU DE TOCQUEVILLE,

August 1850.

CONVERSATIONS.

Journal in Normandy.

Tocqueville, August 16, 1850.—The Château of Tocqueville is built of granite, and parts of it appear to be very ancient, particularly three round towers. One is detached and roofless, but may once have been connected with the body of the castle. Another contains two inhabited stories, besides one on the ground, which looks as if it had been the dungeon; the third is filled by a large winding staircase of granite. The inhabited rooms are principally modern, that is to say, of the time of Louis XIII., and form a very agreeable house.

The Count de Tocqueville offered to his son a much finer castle, Tourlainville, on an eminence about two miles from Cherbourg; but it is a shell, and would have cost 100,000 francs to render it habitable, so the Tocquevilles wisely preferred their present less ambitious residence. Though on high land and not a mile and a half from the sea, it has no sea-view.

At Tocqueville I found, besides M. and Madame Alexis de Tocqueville, his father and his elder brother, with two sons and a daughter. Madame de Tocqueville appears to be quite recovered. She complains, however, of bronchitic affection whenever the weather is damp, and is easily fatigued. Alexis de Tocqueville speaks of himself as well. He can talk as much as he likes, and intends to attend the Conseil général on the 26th, where he will have not only to speak but to debate.

The Count looks like a fine old man of sixty-five or sixty-six, but is really seventy-eight. His hair is white and has been so for the last fifty-seven years, for it was turned in 1793, when he was imprisoned for nine months with six members of his family, and saw them all leave the prison on one afternoon for trial, judgment, and execution. His own trial was fixed for the 10th thermidor. So that if Robespierre's fall had been delayed two days we should have lost ' La Démocratie en Amérique,' and all that we may hope is to follow.

One gets used to everything, even to imminent death. The disagreeable time in every day was about half-past three, when those selected for trial were summoned. The Count accustomed himself to pass from three to four in sleep.

We talked after dinner of the new election law.

Tocqueville said that his Government intended to pass an amended election law, really to effect the purpose which is the pretext of this, the exclusion of the vagabond population. How this will work no one can say. It is so obscurely worded that it receives different interpretations everywhere. The only thing certain is, that it will destroy at least three millions of votes, many of them those which, if the principle of universal suffrage is to be retained, well deserve to be preserved. In Tocqueville, for instance, no heads of families had taken the trouble to register their sons, lodgers, or servants.

All these, probably a majority of the voters, would have been excluded if Tocqueville had not sent round to them papers to be filled up.

August 17.—I talked over with Tocqueville the prospects of the four great parties.

'The terror,' he said, 'which the Republic at first spread has passed off. Men see that it does not necessarily bring with it war, paper currency, and bankruptcy, still less confiscation and the guillotine. But it is not trusted; the feeling of the mass of the people, of the peasant, the artisan, and the shop-keeper, as well as of the proprietor and the merchant, is against a constantly shifting chief. Far from valuing the power of electing a new quasi-king every four years, they detest it. "We must," they say, "have something permanent." The Republican party, therefore, as a party, has become powerless. Two years hence, or perhaps sooner, some different form of government will be established.'

'Will it then be the return of the Orleans family, excluding the elder branch?'

'That seems scarcely possible; their legal claims are no better than those of Changarnier or of Lamartine. All that their friends can say is, that the people have a right to choose their rulers, and would do wisely in choosing *them*. But their friends are a minority, small when compared with the number who are indifferent to them, and not large when compared with the number who are positively hostile to them.'

'Will it be the return of Henri V.?'

'The great obstacle to this is the association of the

Bourbon name with the old *régime*; that Government, gay and brilliant as it looks in our histories and in our memoirs, must have been horribly bad, for the detestation of it is almost the only feeling that has survived the sixty years of revolution that have passed since its fall.

'The French can bear oppression, they can bear to see their children carried off by the conscription, and their property by the tax-gatherer, but they cannot bear the privileges and petty vexations of feudalism. You saw the roofless tower in the court. My grandfather used it as a *colombier*. He kept there 3,000 pigeons. No one was allowed to kill them, and no one else in the commune could keep them. In 1793, when the peasants were the masters, they did no harm to any of the rest of our property. We have lived among them as protectors and friends for centuries—but they rose *en masse* against the pigeons, killed everyone of them, and reduced the tower to its present state. When I first was a candidate I failed, not because I was not personally popular, but because I was *gentilhomme*. I was met everywhere by the proverb: "*Les chats prennent les souris.*" My opponent was of a humble family which had risen to wealth and distinction in the Revolution. This is the most favourable combination in the hands of a man of ability. Mere wealth is mischievous; it gives no influence, and it excites envy. The only time when it led to political power, was just after the revolution of 1848. Every possessor of property, and few persons in the provinces are quite without it, was alarmed. And the greatest proprietors were selected as representatives because they were supposed to have the greatest stakes. Mere birth is still worse than mere wealth; it excites not only envy but fear.

'The remembrance of the Marian persecutions is still vivid in England after 300 years. Our fears of the revival of the *tour et colombier* are as fantastic as your dread of the faggot and the rack; but why should they not last as long?

'Last come the Bonapartists. Will Louis Napoleon succeed in becoming Emperor? I think not; I doubt whether he will attempt it. He is daring in his plans, but when the moment of execution comes he hesitates. His best chance was on January 29, 1849. He then enjoyed the full prestige of his six millions of votes, and his moral and intellectual mediocrity had not been detected. I have no doubt that the plan was laid, but at the decisive moment he, or his advisers, flinched.'

I said that one of his rashest acts seemed to be, the dismissal in November 1849 of the only respectable ministry that could be obtained.

Tocqueville answered that supposing his object to be the establishment of himself as permanent ruler and the subversion of the present Constitution, his conduct then was at least plausible.

'We,' he said, 'had served his purpose. We had enabled him to get through the most perilous period of his new reign, the substitution of the Legislative for the Constituent Assembly. We had maintained peace within and without, but we were doing *too* well. The

Republic was becoming respectable, and there was a fear that the people would acquiesce in it. By throwing the administration into the hands of a set of clerks without experience or authority, he let loose the passions of the Assembly, and enabled it to become, what is not easy, both formidable and contemptible.

'I will not venture to prophesy or even to guess, but I think that the least improbable result is, that he will be re-elected at the end of his time, but, that in other respects, the present Constitution will last its three years : beyond that all is darkness.

'If any event indistinctly presents itself, it is the reconciliation of the two branches, and the success of an united effort to give the crown to Henri V. and to the Comte de Paris as his successor. This is perhaps our best chance now, as the maintenance of the elder branch was our best chance twenty years ago. The almost inconceivable folly of Charles X. and of his advisers or flatterers ruined us then, and perhaps the animosities and jealousies of the two branches may interpose themselves when the next occasion arises. The younger Princes are, we are told, favourable to this arrangement. It would restore them to France, and in a high position.

'The Duchess of Orleans, however, is said to be opposed to it, and no one can tell what will be the conduct five or six years hence of the Comte de Paris.'

As we were going to walk, Rivet arrived from Paris. His news was that the Republican party had almost ceased to exist. He talked on Thursday with

Bergeron, one of their leaders, a revolutionist of 1848, a conspirator of 1849, who had fled to England after the affairs of June. Bergeron told him that his party was all dispersed or demoralised. Many have gone to California, others were engaged in commerce and manufactures.

'If I wanted,' he said, 'an *émeute*, I could not find three persons to raise a paving stone.'

Socialism, too, has ceased to occupy people's minds. Everybody, in short, is tired of even thinking about politics.

He too thinks the re-election of the President the most probable of near events. Much may depend on his present progress. If it should ultimately be considered a failure, he is lost, and such a result is not improbable. Public receptions are not scenes in which he shows to advantage. He can ride well, and looks imposing when he enters a town on horseback, and he can deliver tolerably a speech which he has learned by heart, but in those two things are summed up his powers of acting the king before a crowd. He does not captivate by manner, for he is cold and reserved. His inferiority to the Orleans Princes must strike everyone. Still he is *there*, and he has therefore for him one of the strongest of the present feelings of France—the fear of change.

Sunday, August 18, 1850.—Tocqueville joined me as I was walking before breakfast. He told me that after early mass, the priest had authorised his parishioners to spend the day in getting in their harvest—only advising them to cherish pious thoughts while doing so. This led us to talk of the general state of religion in France.

'In the last century,' said Tocqueville, 'religion had almost ceased among the higher classes, and incredulity, beginning with them, had spread to the middle and even to the lower classes.

'The Revolution of 1789 changed the feelings of the aristocracy, they connected irreligion with democracy, and tried to revive Christianity as a political engine. To do this it was necessary to appear to believe it, at least to treat it with respect. And accordingly no gentleman in the present century writes, or even speaks, irreligiously. The lower and middle classes however, who have been gainers by the Revolution, felt rather grateful to scepticism for its assistance. They were led by the conduct of Louis XVIII. and his courtiers to connect religion with aristocracy, and to impute to those who affected the one a desire to bring back the other. The revolution of 1830 was almost as anti-religious as it was anti-legitimist.

'Christianity was less hated by the *bourgeoisie* under Louis Philippe, than it had been under Charles X., because it was less dreaded, but it was quite as much despised. 1848, however, by dethroning the middle classes, has converted them. They too see the want of the religious sanction ; they now wish to join the aristocracy in imposing its restraints on the people.

'None but the lowest classes now profess irreligion. All the higher and all the middle classes are anxious to promote and to extend Christianity.'

I said that it did not seem to me that a political faith of this kind would do much. That it might produce an outward surface of respect and even of conformity, covering general unbelief.

Tocqueville answered that he did not believe that such a surface would cover *general* unbelief. That the instinct which leads the mass of mankind to assume the existence and the influence of a supernatural Being is so strong that it will always prevail unless it is violently opposed. That a religious system which is taught in every school, preached from every pulpit, and treated by all the educated portion of society as if it were true, will be received without examination by nine-tenths of those to whom it is offered, and adopted and retained by them without suspicion. Many of his friends, men of intelligence and learning, are undoubting Catholics. Falloux is an example. A man of high talents and acquirements and virtues, who, much against his will, took office, because his confessor told him that it was his duty.

I said that there were duties imposed by Catholicism so disagreeable that I should be unable to undergo them, and being unable to conform without submitting to them, I should break loose.

'Certainly,' he said, 'many of our observances are painful, and on some minds they produce the effect they would on you, but to many others the very irksomeness is an incentive. They estimate the merit by the disagreeableness. They delight in the idea that they are performing palpable, measurable, countable good works —that they are laying up a treasure in Heaven, of which the amount can be calculated, and for which the security is perfect.'

After breakfast the Count, Alexis de Tocqueville, his nephew and his niece, and I visited the four principal farmhouses of the estate. There are no ricks in this country, everything is housed, and the farm-buildings therefore are enormous—to the great detriment of the landlord, who has to keep them up. They are constructed of granite, but thatched, and seem to require no rebuilding but frequent repairs. All looked as if they had existed for centuries, during several of which they may have been gentlemen's houses. One was pointed out to me as the *berceau* or traditional first residence of the De Tocquevilles.

All had the untidiness which belongs to the agricultural classes of France. The farmyards were unlevelled and full of pools of water and manure. The kitchen of every house, apparently the only sitting-room, and, in two cases, serving as the best bedroom, was much in the same state: its floor was merely an extension of the farmyard. The people were exceedingly civil and kind, but perfectly unformed. Their manners in general were more uncouth than those of our labourers. Their great effort was to persuade us to keep on our hats in their rooms ; to effect which they usually set us the example. Some of the girls were exceedingly handsome. In the first that we visited we found all the family—parents, children, and servants—just finishing their dinner, probably about twenty persons. I could perceive no distinction in manners or dress. By far the most

civilised person was a very pretty maid-servant. The
master of this house occupied 200 verges, or 100 acres,
for which he paid 5,000 francs a year. The taxes,
however, both general and local, are paid by the landlord, and they are heavy in this part of Normandy;
not less than a quarter of the rent.

The next farm was of the same extent, but rented at
only 3,000 francs. The occupier has an estate of his
own of about equal value. His son is at the college of
Valognes, and will be an *avocat*. I was struck by the
number of children. One farmer had seven; another
had nine. This is very unusual in France, where the
children to a marriage average only three. Tocqueville
told me that in this class of life children are wealth.
The sons seldom marry or leave their father's house till
they are nearly forty, or the girls till they are long past
thirty. In the meantime they are by far the best labourers that he can have. The name applied to a girl amused
me. It is '*créature*.' If you ask a peasant what family
he has, he answers perhaps that he has two *garçons* and
three *créatures*.

With all their rudeness they are said to be excellent
cultivators, as may be inferred from the high rents which
they pay. Their horses and cattle are fine. One
farm only appeared to have a waggon. In the others
the harvest was being carried home on a sort of cradle
placed on a horse's back and supporting six sheaves on
each side. Twenty years ago no other mode of conveyance was possible, for what were called roads were
mere lanes just broad enough to admit a horse and its

burden. In the coach-house of the castle I saw the old family carriage. It is the body of a *vis-à-vis* supported by four shafts extending before and behind like a large bath-chair, only that two horses carried it instead of men.

The capital necessary to a farm is supposed to be about 3*l*. or 4*l*. an acre. In Picardy, or the Isle of France, it is much more. There a farm of 300 acres would require a capital of 4,000*l*. The Métayer system is unknown. All the land is cultivated by its owner or farmed.

The whole of this estate contains about 1,200 verges, or 600 acres, and is worth about 1,000 francs a verge or 80*l*. an acre. This would be a high value with us, especially in a district remote from the capital and from any great town. The land, however, is eminently fertile, and the seaweed called *vanecque* is an excellent manure always at hand. Rivet estimated the annual value at 25,000 francs. Tocqueville said that it was rather more. Farm wages are thirty sous a day, or nine francs a week. On these wages it is supposed that a man can support himself, a wife, and three children unable to earn anything. If he have more he requires assistance. The labourer's cottage is generally his own.

Here, as in the rest of France, there is distress among the landlords and tenants. There is much arrear of rent, and it is difficult to relet a farm that is on hand. Agriculture is the only industry that has not recovered from the revolution of 1848. I cannot understand this. One solution is the enormous harvests of 1848 and 1849, which have lowered the price more than in proportion to the excess of quantity; but this would not affect cattle, which have fallen as much as corn.

Another is want of confidence in the existing institutions which stops agricultural improvements. This might affect the labourer by lessening the demand for labour, but not the other classes. Tocqueville says that consumption has diminished, not indeed of bread, but of meat. This is a real, but not an adequate cause. The fact however, whatever be the explanation, is certain. 'Were it otherwise,' said Tocqueville, 'my neighbours would not complain of the Republic.'

This is a breeding country, but horses are dear. A very good hack costs from 1,800 to 2,000 francs. The Government imports stallions, and supplies good ones at a low price, but the farmers, farmer-like, will not attend to the selection of the dams. Still the breed is improving.

That of the Limousin country is becoming extinct, in consequence of the extension of enclosures. It was originally Arab, and very active and persevering. A good Limousin horse now costs about 1,800 francs.

At Bayeux I saw posted up the programme of the Races of the Department for the 25th of next September. The prizes are given by the Government and as high as 2,500 francs. All the horses were to be stallions, born in France, and not less than four years old. At an older age they were to be weighted proportionately. The contests were not confined to galloping. Some were for trotting, and others for drawing.

This is a more sensible racing system than ours.

Monday, August 19, 1850.—The Count de Tocqueville left us this morning.

As I was going out of the gate before breakfast, I met a professional beggar entering with his wallet on his back. Strangers receive a sou, but on only one day in the week. The poor belonging to the parish are relieved with food by the Tocquevilles, and by the farmers, and sometimes with money. I saw the Count give the *curé* a five-franc piece for a particular case. There is no collection in the church, nor any regular fund for the poor. All is left to private charity.

Tocqueville took me a long walk along the side of a valley traversed by a stream which turns three mills. The land is his and might be converted into excellent water meadow. It is now neglected, and merely used by the millers to pasture their horses.

Tocqueville says that if things were in a settled state, he should set to work to improve it.

We talked of Thiers's 'History of the Empire.'

Tocqueville said that it disappointed him. He expected more from so good a speaker and so admirable a converser. It is too long and too detailed. What do we care whether the Duke of Dalmatia marched on a given point by one path or by another? These are positive faults. Its negative defect is its inadequate appreciation of the causes, intrinsic and extrinsic, which united to form Napoleon.

'Few histories,' said Tocqueville, 'give to these two sets of causes their due, or their relative weight. Some attribute too much to the circumstances in which their hero is placed, others to the accidents of his character. Napoleon, though gigantic in war and in legislation, was imperfect and incoherent in both. No other great general, perhaps no other general whatever, suffered so many defeats. Many have lost one army, some perhaps have lost two, but who ever survived the destruction of four? So in legislation: he subdued anarchy, he restored our finances, he did much to which France owes in part her power and her glory. But he deprived her not only of liberty, but of the wish for liberty; he enveloped her in a network of centralisation, which stifles individual and corporate resistance, and prepares the way for the despotism of an Assembly or of an Emperor. Assuming him to have been perfectly selfish, nothing could be better planned, or better executed. He seized with a sagacity which is really marvellous, out of the elements left to him by the Convention, those which enabled him to raise *himself*, and to level everything else; which enabled his will to penetrate into the recesses of provincial and even of private life, and rendered those below him incapable of acting and thinking, almost of wishing, for themselves. All this is very inadequately shown by Thiers. He does not sufficiently explain how it was that Napoleon was able to do this, or, why it was that he chose to do it. Nor has his private character been ever well drawn as a whole.

'There is much truth in Bourrienne, though mixed, and inseparably mixed, with much invention. Napoleon's taste was defective in everything, in small things as well as in great ones; in books, in art, and in women, as well as in ambition and in glory; and his idolizers cannot be men of much better taste. The History of the Empire and the History of the Emperor are still to be written. I hope one day to write them.'

We drove afterwards to St. Pierre, an estate belonging to Madame de Blangy, a cousin of Tocqueville's. She is an old lady of seventy-five, and lives there with her son, Gaston de Blangy.

It formerly belonged to the family of St. Pierre, the author of the project of universal peace, and was sold to the Blangy's forty years ago for a trifling price, about 4,000*l*.

The family were absent, and we wandered over the park and château. The building is a vast parallelogram quite regular, and very ugly, and, as it is composed of blocks of granite, its ugliness will probably endure for centuries. It stands on a plateau about a mile from the sea, more than half way up the ridge of a hill, which all along this peninsula overlooks the coast. The sea-views therefore are fine. The park is extensive and perfectly French, the greater part of it covered by trees thickly planted and never thinned, and therefore tall and boughless. In the midst of this artificial forest are patches of cultivated ground, and it is pierced by long avenues some running up the hill, and others opening on the sea. Such combinations, though they may not be natural, are grand and imposing.

We talked of the life in English country-houses.

'I cannot understand,' said Tocqueville, 'how your

great people, after having passed six months of representation in London, like to create a little London for themselves in the country. *We* never think of filling our country-houses with crowds of acquaintances. Our parties are mere family parties, and all our arrangements are meant for ease and comfort. There is no luxury or display in our furniture, no ostentation in our dinners.'

I answered, that the presence of a large party at a country-house is the exception; that a man who can afford it fills his house for four or five weeks, and then lives with only his family, or some intimate friends, for a month or two. And that there is a motive for inviting our friends in England which is wanting in France. In Paris, where the town is comparatively small, the distances near, the persons who form a set not numerous, and everybody's evenings disengaged from business, there is much intimacy. Those who like one another's society can obtain it habitually. In London, where one has to go three or four miles to see one's friends, where the names in a visiting book are counted by hundreds, where few busy men can spare more than one or two evenings in a week, one scarcely sees the persons that one likes best a dozen times in a season, and then perhaps it is at a large dinner, or in a crowded party. One can really enjoy their society only in the country.

From the park we went to the stables, which are large and lofty. There were several fine horses. One, a mare, was thirty years old, another had won several prizes. M. de Blangy, some years ago, set to work to improve the breed of the district. He imported stallions and mares, established races, and has at length so far succeeded as to be often beaten. He is also a great agricultural improver, and notwithstanding his high birth, might represent the department, if he did not systematically abstain from politics.

The curé dined with us. He is about thirty-five, tall, rather thin, very decent and well behaved. He did not seem embarrassed, but took scarcely any part in the conversation at dinner or in the drawing-room. This, Tocqueville said, was *convenable*.

We talked of the paucity of modern great men. A few names were suggested. One was Sir Robert Peel. 'Peel,' I said, 'certainly did great things, and the last four years of his life were useful and dignified; but his character, both moral and intellectual, was too imperfect for greatness.

'He had a clear perception, for instance, for what was expedient for the moment. He could conjecture, perhaps, what would be necessary in six months to come,—but he could not foresee for a year. It is impossible to believe that when in 1828 he denounced Catholic Emancipation as fatal, he thought it possible that in 1829 he should have to support it himself. When he turned out the Whigs for proposing free trade in 1841, he could not have supposed that he should have to bring it forward in 1845. He was very clear-sighted, but very short-sighted. Then, as to his public spirit. No one certainly made greater sacrifices to patriotism. He threw away for the sake of his country, honour and truth. He submitted to the misery of wearing a mask for years, and to the shame of throwing it off.

'On no other terms, perhaps, could he have carried his great measures. But a man who will use such means, can scarcely be called great. And though the fear of civil war forced him ultimately to assist in repealing the Catholics' disabilities, and the fear of famine, perhaps of revolution, forced him ultimately to repeal the corn laws, he supported those institutions long after he must have perceived them to be mischievous. His doing this was evidence of moral defects. His not perceiving sooner the extent of their mischief was an intellectual defect.'

Washington and Wellington were proposed. The moral merits of each were admitted, and the possession by each of good sense in the highest degree; but they were denied genius.

With respect to the Duke of Wellington, Tocqueville acknowledged his greatness as a general. He ought not, perhaps, to be put on a par with Cæsar, or Alexander, or Hannibal, but he was fully equal to Turenne; but he doubted his greatness as a statesman. He believed that his advice in 1815 had been mistaken, and his influence mischievous.

'His English career as a statesman,' I answered, 'though disfigured by some great errors, was useful and even glorious. The manner in which he carried Catholic Emancipation was a masterpiece of decision, energy, and skill. Perhaps we owe to him the existence of the House of Lords. Under guidance less wise and less firm than his, that House might have dashed itself to pieces against the House of Commons in the storms of the Grey and Melbourne administrations.' We afterwards got to smaller people—Soult, Bugeaud, and Lamoricière.

I asked what sort of a statesman Soult was.

'Nothing,' said Rivet,' 'could be weaker than his character as a politician, nothing more admirable than his skill as an administrator. All who know anything of the war department will tell you that he was the greatest minister of war we ever had.'

.' Bugeaud,' said Tocqueville, ' with all his weaknesses and vanity, had many of the elements of greatness. His courage amounted to heroism, and it was political as well as military. He had more public spirit than is often found in this narrow-minded generation. And his care of his soldiers was exemplary. When I was with him in Algiers, I saw how carefully he examined every detail. His officers did not much like him, but he was adored by the men.'

Both the Tocquevilles and Rivet were surprised to hear from me that Bugeaud had cherished hopes of the Presidentship. I have seen a letter in his own hand in which he gave instructions as to the mode in which he wished to be brought forward as a candidate.

Lamoricière seemed to be the favourite of everybody. Madame de Tocqueville praised his wit and his conversation. He has lived so un-Parisian a life that it is all original. Tocqueville spoke of his powers of application. He can work from dinner-time to two in the morning without fatigue. He is killing himself, however, by smoking. The cigar is literally never out of his mouth. Rivet went to see him on February 25, 1848. He was lying incapable of moving from exhaustion, fatigue, and scratches from bayonets. All he could do was to smoke.

'When Lamoricière,' said Tocqueville, 'went to Petersburg in 1848, a friend of mine, an eminent professor, travelled with him for the first day. My friend, with his professional habits, lectured him on what he should say to Nicholas. "Tell him," he said, "that he has nothing to fear from the Republic; that we wish to interfere with nobody, and merely to be allowed to settle our own affairs in our own way; and that if he will leave us quiet, we shall be delighted to be his friends." When Lamoricière returned, he said to me, "Well, I delivered our friend's message to the Czar, and he answered, 'My good friend, there was no need to tell me all this: I have not the least wish to interfere with you. Whether you have a Republic, or a Dictator, or an Emperor, I do not care a rouble. The only government that I cannot tolerate is a Constitutional Monarchy, and in your case I see no immediate danger of *that*.'"'

Tuesday, August 20.—Tocqueville, Rivet, and I rode along the coast. We talked of a subject which has lately much engaged Rivet—the mode of recruiting the army. The French army now consists of about 80,000 men in Algiers, and 300,000 in France. Of these 380,000 men, about 80,000 are *remplaçants* who have been attracted into the service as substitutes, 16,000 are volunteers, and the rest are conscripts. It serves for seven years. Of these three elements the *remplaçants*, though they serve for the longest period, are the worst. This seems to be partly the consequence of the treatment which they receive. Their companions look down on them as mercenaries who serve, not as paying the debt which they owe to their country but for money, and they are refused promotion. Next to them are the volunteers, and far superior to the rest are the conscripts. The best soldier is the conscript taken from the plough.

About 7,000 punishments are inflicted every year, of which, 5,800 fall on the 96,000 *remplaçants* and volunteers, and only 1,200 on the 284,000 conscripts. France is called a military nation, but never, in her utmost need, or when, as in 1848, distress among the labouring classes has been general, have the voluntary enlistments exceeded 24,000 in a year. The remedy would be an increase of pay or of bounty; but this is forbidden by the state of the finances. The budget of the army is already enormous.

I asked what amount of first-rate troops would be sufficient to maintain order in France.

Tocqueville said that a permanent army of 150,000 men well paid and disciplined, the members of which adopted it as a profession, would be more than enough.

'Then why not substitute it for the 300,000 ill-disciplined troops that you keep there now?'

'Because,' he answered, 'with an army of only

150,000 men, we should be unable to make war, and the nation would think itself betrayed. The power, and under certain circumstances the willingness, to make war, is the first duty which the nation requires from its Government. The great complaint against Louis Philippe—the fault which most produced his overthrow, was the belief that he was incurably pacific. With much less than 400,000 men, we cannot make war. What we hope to do is, to give to the Government the duty and the monopoly of finding substitutes, to take them out of the 55,000 men that are every year disbanded, and to make the service of *remplaçants* honourable by selecting them as a reward from among the best-conducted men. But while Germany and Russia remain armed, we cannot materially reduce our army, and until we materially reduce it, we cannot render it attractive by increase of bounty or pay.'

I asked for an outline of the new law on education.

'Anybody,' they said, 'wishing to open a school must apply to the Maire of the Commune, and produce testimony of his fitness. If no objection be made for a month, he may open it, and except that his school is inspected from time to time by persons appointed by the Government, he is subject to little interference. If his application be refused by the Maire, or objected to by the Commune, an appeal lies to a Court in the chef lieu of the department of which the Bishop and the Prefect are members: the same tribunal can close a school that has been complained of.'

This is the law which has been introduced by the

Clergy, and is attacked as throwing all education into their hands.

It appears to me a reasonable one. All schools are subject to inspection, and the superintending it is a considerable branch of the duties of the Minister of Public Instruction.

I asked how the École Polytechnique was filled.

'By public competition,' answered Tocqueville. 'Every year there are about 120 vacancies, for which there are about 1,200 candidates. The severity of the competition injures the health of many of the candidates, and the prize, after all, is scarcely to be desired.

'The education is rather scientific than practical. They come out of it *des bêtes savantes*. The prizes, however, which it offers are considerable. It is the only avenue to the Ponts et Chaussées, the mining department, the engineers and artillery. The pupils are revolutionists while there, but their education seems little to affect their subsequent politics. Its defect is, that it does not fit them for the world.'

At dinner we talked of the society of the country. When Paris could be reached only by a journey of eight or nine days, Valognes, a small town about fifteen miles off, was the provincial metropolis. All the country-gentlemen had houses there, in which they passed the winter. The Comte de Tocqueville sold his some years ago. The *noblesse* and *bourgeoisie*, however, formed then, indeed form now, distinct societies. The only place of amusement in which they met was a concert-room. A friend of Madame de Tocqueville proposed, a year or two ago, to give a ball to both sets. The noble ladies sent her word that their husbands might go, but that they should not. She persisted, and so did they, and as far as ladies were concerned the ball was *bourgeois*.

When Alexis de Tocqueville entered his name on the roll of *avocats*, with the intention of pursuing the judicial career, his noble friends at Valognes were scandalised. 'Your ancestors,' they said to him, 'were always gens de l'épée, et vous portez la robe.'

We passed to the subject of Marriage. In the higher classes they are usually marriages *de convenance*, and indeed must be so, as young ladies go out but little, and it is not the practice to talk much. On the female side they are generally early; a girl unmarried at twenty-one or twenty-two gets alarmed. She frequently takes to devotion—dislikes dancing and the theatre, and is very regular at mass. On her marriage, however, the relapse into the world is instantaneous. From a *vieille fille* she turns into a *jeune femme*—from a grub into a butterfly. There are several reasons for this interval of devotion. The *curés* are the principal marriage-makers. They alone know everybody. A man of eight or nine and twenty may wish for a wife, but is too busy or too awkward to set about getting one for himself. He applies to the *curé*, tells him perhaps that he has twenty or twenty-five thousand francs a year. 'Well,' answers the *curé*, 'I think that I have three or four charming demoiselles at about that price.' So the introduction is managed, and the affair is concluded in a few weeks.

'The life of an unmarried girl,' said Madame de Tocqueville, 'is very *triste*. She never quits her mother's side except perhaps to dance, and then does not exchange a word with her partner; she takes no part in conversation; she effaces herself, in short, as much as possible. Were she to do otherwise she would ruin her chances of marriage.'

Wednesday, August 21, 1850.—At six o'clock this morning we set off for Cherbourg, to see a rehearsal of the naval review which is to be given to the President a fortnight hence, and to go over the Arsenal.

Tocqueville and his nephews and niece filled one carriage, Rivet and I another.

On the road we talked of the party to which Tocqueville belongs, of which Dufaure, Beaumont, and Lanjuinais are the principal members.

Tocqueville's talents and knowledge, and courage and character, seem to point him out for the leader. But, in the first place, he wants physical strength. As a consequence of that want he has never practised the constant debating which is required from the head of a party. And, secondly, he is intolerant of mediocrity. He will not court, or talk over, or even listen to, the commonplace men who form the rank and file of every Assembly; he scarcely knows their names. The leadership, therefore, has fallen to Dufaure, or rather has been forced on him. He is an admirable speaker, and has shown great skill in the management of the Assembly; but he is diffident and seems almost afraid to take the lead that is offered to him.

Lanjuinais is a man of high character, and his opinions on the subjects which he has considered are clear and precise and generally just.

Beaumont has not yet become a fluent speaker, though he has spoken well occasionally. His diplomatic absences have put him out of practice, but his talents and knowledge must force him on, and they are aided by his popularity. Never was there a more delightful companion. He must have astonished, however, his colleagues in London and Vienna.

His vehemence, his *brusquerie*, his *abandon* are charming, but not quite diplomatic.

Rivet thinks that Tocqueville would be happier in public than in private life. And I suspect that he thinks so himself.

'What I regret,' he said to me the other day, 'of my ministerial functions is the labour and the absorption. I delighted in not having a moment of the day to myself. I am naturally, perhaps, melancholy, and when it has nothing else to do, my mind preys on itself.'

The rain began to fall as we started, and by the time we reached Cherbourg it became a regular wet day. We were to have left the pier in the boat of the ' Henri Quatre' at a quarter after nine, but instead of a boat came a message to say that the review is put off till tomorrow. The messenger brought us all sorts of tickets for the yards and forts, but the weather has been so pertinaciously bad that we have stayed in the hotel overlooking the basin, and the last sixteen pages of my journal have been the result on my part. It is now about half-past four. M. Hippolyte de Tocqueville, whose château, Nacqueville, is about four miles off, has begged us to spend the evening there, and we are going as soon as Alexis de Tocqueville has paid a few visits to constituents.

Wednesday evening, August 21.—Nacqueville is beautifully placed half way up a long wooded valley rising from the sea. A stream runs through the valley which has been dammed, and forms a lake just below the château, and is crossed opposite to it by a bridge and an ancient castellated barbican which they barbarously call a postern. The château itself is an old granite house of the fourteenth or fifteenth century, with a high roof and square stone windows, which the Hippolyte de Tocquevilles have converted into a large comfortable residence.

On a smaller scale the place itself and the scenery about resemble Glenarm, in Ireland. So indeed does the climate. Though in the middle of August we were glad to find a fire. We have never been without one at Tocqueville.

The evening was very agreeable. The whole Tocqueville family, except Édouard and his wife, were present, and *they* were represented by their sons and daughters, very pleasing young people.

Thursday, August 22.—The windows of my bedroom looked up the valley on one side, and caught a side view of the sea on the other.

We left Nacqueville at six this morning, and returned to Cherbourg. On our way we visited the Arsenal militaire. It is a large fortified enclosure containing an arsenal, a dockyard, a floating basin, and two artificial harbours. The second or inner harbour is now in process of formation, by blasting the rock which, in the neighbourhood of Cherbourg, lies immediately under the surface, and creating a square of about twenty acres in extent, and fifty feet deep, in which at low tide there will be thirty feet of water. The outer harbour is of the same depth, but appeared to me to be about half the size. This was the harbour which was opened on August 27, 1813, in the presence of Maria Louisa—as Napoleon was marching towards his fall in Russia. It employed 1,500 men and 400 horses for ten years, and cost 17,400,000 francs, about 700,000*l.* The floating dock, dry dock, and four covered slips, each large enough to build a three-decker, were constructed during the Restoration—the slips are gigantic absurdities. Each is surrounded by walls and arches of granite, which would carry the tubular bridge over the Menai, and really support only a light timber roof. The dry dock, in which ships of the line were to be repaired, is placed so high as to be accessible to them only at the equinoctial high tides.

After breakfast we went on board the 'Friedland,' a three-decker, of 120 guns, carrying the admiral's flag. The men were exercised with the musket and cutlass, in boarding and repelling boarders, and this was followed by a cannonade by the whole fleet. The pieces recoiled little, but the poop, on which we stood, shook with every discharge. The effect was fine. The flashes in the midst of the white smoke, and the gradual rolling away of the smoke along the sea, were very striking.

It was not comparable, however, to a cannonade which I once witnessed in the Bay of Genoa. I was on board a frigate, on each side of which were two others. It was a dark night, and every discharge from the guns which were opposed to us looked like the eruption of a volcano.

We then rowed to the Digue, and walked nearly a mile and a half from its centre to the western extremity. It is finished as a breakwater, though the forts which are to crown each end are not yet constructed. The roadstead which it encloses cannot contain less than a couple of square miles, but the bottom is rock and the depth unequal. Still it is supposed to afford safe anchorage for sixty-five ships of the line, and, as respects smaller vessels, for more than France possesses.

It will not, however, be much frequented by merchantmen. Cherbourg, placed at the extremity of a narrow peninsula, and with Havre for its rival, can never have much trade. It is valuable merely as a weapon against England. For this purpose France has spent on it, during the last sixty years, about nine millions sterling, and probably will spend one or two millions more. Had the difficulty of the execution, or even the amount of the expenditure been foreseen, it is probable that it would not have been attempted; but Tocqueville thinks that the money has been well laid out. Its influence in a naval war will be great, greater perhaps than it is easy to estimate.

Hitherto we have been able to blockade every French port. Cherbourg alone will be a refuge without being a prison. Its coast is too dangerous and its sea too stormy to be constantly blockaded, and having both an eastern and a western outlet, there are few winds in which it cannot be quitted.

A large fleet, as large as France can man, may be united or even built behind its fortifications, and be there safe, but ready to start at a moment's notice, for battle, or plunder, or invasion.

It will be joined to Paris by the Chartres Railway, and perhaps by that of Rouen, for each of them proposes to have a branch to Caen. The different Governments under whose direction it has been completed, have each buried among its works inscriptions containing their titles and their self-gratulations.

'If ever,' said Tocqueville, 'some convulsion of Nature should uncover the deep foundations of the port of Cherbourg, the vestiges of five different dynasties will be revealed, each of which has deposited there a memorial of its power, of its confidence, and of its instability.'

We returned to Tocqueville by six o'clock. A *curé* from the neighbourhood dined with us. He was older and more familiar than the *curé* of Tocqueville.

The conversation turned on learned women: he repeated the Norman proverb, 'Prêtre qui danse, poule qui chante, et femme qui parle Latin, ne sont bons à rien.'

After dinner we talked over the Revolution of 1848.

'One of its conditions,' said Tocqueville, 'was the substitution which we made in 1844 of open voting for the ballot. Nothing but open voting kept Guizot in power from 1845 to 1848. And yet Duchâtel was opposed to the change.

'Guizot was wiser. Another of its conditions was the dismissal of Guizot neither before nor after February 23. If Louis Philippe had turned him out a week sooner, or had kept him in a week longer, he would still have been on the throne. I had a long conversation with one of the ministers about a week before. I was alarmed, but he laughed at my fears. "There is no cause," he said, "even for uneasiness; there are 65,000 troops in Paris besides the National Guards."

'In fact, however, there were only 25,000; but that was more than enough if they had been allowed to act. As soon, however, as Louis Philippe heard that the National Guards were wavering he despaired.

'There is not a more revolutionary institution,' he continued, 'that is to say, an institution more productive of revolutions, than a National Guard. Just after a revolution, to be sure, it is useful as a protector of property, but its instincts are to bring one on. The majority of its members have no political knowledge, they sympathise with the prevalent feeling, which is seldom favourable to a Government; some wish to give it a lesson, others would like to overthrow it; very few, except in moments of excitement, like those of June 1848, choose to expose themselves in its defence; and one National Guard who joins the mob does more harm than all the good that can be done by twenty who support the Government. The mob have not the least respect for the uniform, but the soldiers will not fire on it.

'Even on February 24,' continued Tocqueville, 'the Monarchy might have been saved if the proclamation of the Provisional Government and the retreat of the Duchess of Orleans could have been retarded one hour. After having sat out the revolutionary scene, heard the proclamation of the Republic, and seen Lamartine and Ledru Rollin set off for the Hôtel de Ville, I. was quitting the Chamber, and had reached the landing-place of the staircase which leads from the waiting-room into the court now occupied by our Provisional House, when I met a company of the 10th Legion, with fixed bayonets, led by General Oudinot, not in uniform, but brandishing his cane in a military style, and crying "En avant! Vive le Roi, et la Duchesse d'Orléans Régente!" By his side, gesticulating and shouting in the same manner, was a man[1] whom I will not name, who by the evening had become a fierce Republican. The National Guards, though not numerous, uttered the same cries, and rushed up the staircase with great resolution. Oudinot recognised me; caught me by the arm and cried, "Where are you going? Come with us and we will sweep these ruffians out of the Chamber." "My dear General," I answered, "it is too late; the Chamber is dissolved, the Duchess has fled, the Provisional Government is on its way to the Hôtel de Ville." The impulse, however, which he had given to the column of National Guards

---

[1] Lamartine.—ED.

was such that it did not stop. I turned back, and we all re-entered the Chamber. The crowd had just left it. The National Guards stood still for an instant, looking with astonishment on the empty benches, and then dispersed in all directions. They belonged to the Quartier St. Germain. Oudinot had collected them by going from house to house. If he had been able to do so two hours, or even one hour earlier, the destinies of France, and perhaps of Europe, might have been altered.'

Rivet recalled to Tocqueville's recollection a meeting of the moderate party on the Sunday morning, at which it was resolved to endeavour to persuade the leaders of the opposition to abandon the banquet. The great events which immediately followed had quite obscured it in Tocqueville's memory, but he gradually called it to mind. The result was that Rivet was sent as spokesman to Odillon Barrot and Duvergier de Hausanne; Odillon Barrot acquiesced without much difficulty, but Duvergier de Hausanne resisted, so that their attempt failed. It was only the next morning, after seeing the programme for their proceedings which the newspapers had invented for them in the night, that those who promoted the banquet gave it up.

Rivet was present, or nearly present, at the fatal fire on the Boulevard des Capucins. Its immediate effect has been exaggerated. He saw a band of most sinister-looking ruffians make their way towards the Affaires Étrangères, and foresaw that something would happen. Immediately afterwards there was a discharge, and he and his friend were enveloped in a wave of fugitives which carried them up to the Rue Richelieu, but there did not appear in those around him much exasperation.

La Grange denies that he was present, and he may be believed. The transaction was not one in which he would be ashamed to claim a part.

Friday, August 23.—After breakfast we walked along the plateau behind the house, which commands on three sides the plain extending to the sea, dotted over with church towers which seem to rise from a forest, scooped into deep bays, and extending into promontories, each of which has its old castle or its lighthouse, and washed by a sea, which to-day was blue as the Mediterranean. The defect of this magnificent view is the absence of ships. France appears to have little coasting-trade; and no one, except from necessity, approaches these reefs.

Reverting to our conversation of yesterday, Tocqueville said, that though the revolution of 1848 was a surprise, the existing state of things would not have long continued. The *pays légal*, the 200,000 persons who paid 200 francs of contribution, could not have been allowed much longer to govern absolutely thirty-five millions.

'Never,' he continued, 'was a Government built on narrower or on shallower foundations. It did not rest on numbers, or on wealth, or on education, or on antiquity, or on prejudice, or on respect. It was despised by the lower classes, and detested as well as despised by the higher classes. Few of those whom in England you would call gentry were Orleanists. Most of the persons belonging to the aristocracy were real Legitimists, by feeling as well as by education, and the rest had rallied round the Restoration as the only power which had a past or a future.

'Louis Philippe's conduct was not forgiven. As Regent in the name of Henri V. he might have stood between the throne and the people as effectually as he did as King. By condescending to be the founder of a usurping dynasty, by recognising the right of a Parisian mob to be a setter up and puller down of kings, he set one of the few precedents which are absolutely certain to be followed.

'Sooner or later the Orleans dynasty must have been upset, even if it had reposed on a really democratic basis. But it rested on the most selfish and grasping of plutocracies. There were no nomination seats for the nobles; no scot and lot boroughs for the agitators; no venal ones for the millionnaires; the road to power lay along one flat level terrace of *bourgeoisie*, looked up to with envy and dislike by the multitude below it; and looked down on with scorn amounting to disgust by the better born and better educated classes above it. The *pays légal* were the electors and the elected. They were the donors and the receivers of office and of patronage.

'They made the laws as deputies, they applied them as administrators, and their legislation and their administration were a series of jobs for their own party interests, or for those of their handful of constituents. Their whole conduct excited suspicion, contempt, envy— in short, every hostile passion, except fear. Such a

Government was doomed. Its destruction in 1848 was an accident, but sooner or later some such accident was inevitable.'

I asked what he thought of the system of paid representatives.

'Both the Government,' he said, 'and the people dislike it. The Government because it renders the members independent. The people because they cannot understand the necessity of paying a man to do what he is anxious to do without being paid. But I do not see how we can do without it. It may be abolished, but it will be resumed. Unless the representatives are paid they must be allowed to hold office. With the feelings of our people the greater part of those who will be elected will be poor men. They will not starve with supreme power in their hands. They will force the public to pay them as functionaries if it does not as representatives. But a Chamber of officials would be distrusted by the people. They would be believed, probably with justice, to be the tools of the Executive.'

He prefers on the whole the new system of departmental or collective voting. Under the old system, according to which one electoral body, averaging about 500 persons, returned one deputy, the deputy in fact bought all his constituents, and paid for them out of the public purse. He got for every elector the little place that he wanted at the expense merely of voting with the Minister. Neither the present English plan of buying votes at 10*l.* a-head, nor Sir Robert Walpole's old habit of asking a member to dinner, and putting bank notes or lottery tickets under his plate, was adopted, but it was not less a system of organised corruption. To have got rid of this is a great thing, to force these democratic electors to select men enjoying at least notoriety is another advantage, and a still greater one is the candidate's independence on any individual elector.

We afterwards talked of the subdivision of property. I said that it did not appear to me probable that it was progressive; that with a population slowly increasing as that of France, there must be nearly as much coalition as separation, and that agricultural improvement must more than compensate for any slight augmentation in the number of properties. Tocqueville agreed with me.

'The tendency,' he said, 'is to create farms of the size which one family can *cultivate*, which much exceeds the quantity of land necessary to feed one family. Almost every peasant has his own house; on this beginning he tries, by investing all his savings in land, to add more and more, till he reaches the limit which I have mentioned. Frequently he borrows the money, and that is one of our dangers. The enormous mortgages which oppress our landed interest, comprising three-fourths of our population, create a formidable revolutionary party. It is pretty clear that the first act of a république rouge would be, directly or indirectly, to destroy mortgage debts. Such a Government might not live six months, but it might do this in six days. It might simply apply the sponge, and declare all mortgages void; or it might make its paper a legal tender, and lend it at one per cent. to everyone who offered what it would call a moral security—that is, to every applicant whatever.

'And the next Government would find it difficult to avoid ratifying the acts of its predecessor, or to annul repayments which had been made with a currency legal, however depreciated.'

Saturday, August 25, 1850.—Tocqueville, Rivet, and I took a long walk over the downs commanding the sea.

'I am now forty-five,' said Tocqueville, 'and the change which has taken place in the habits of society, as I faintly recollect my boyhood, seem to have required centuries. The whole object of those among whom I was brought up was to amuse and be amused. Politics were never talked of, and I believe very little thought of. Literature was one of the standing subjects of conversation. Every new book of any merit was read aloud and canvassed and criticised with an attention and a detail which we should now think a deplorable waste of time. I recollect how everybody used to be in ecstasy about things of De Lille's which nothing would tempt me now to look at. Every considerable country-house had its theatre, and its society often furnished admirable actors. I remember my father returning after a short absence to a large party in his house. We amused ourselves by receiving him in disguise. Chateaubriand was an old woman. Nobody would take so much trouble now. Every incident was matter for a little poem.

'People studied the means of pleasing as they now do those which produce profit or power. *Causer* and *raconter* are among the lost arts. So is *tenir salon*. Madame Récamier was the delight of Paris, but she said very little; she listened and smiled intelligently, and from time to time threw in a question or a remark to show that she understood you. From long habit she knew what were the subjects on which each guest showed to most advantage, and she put him upon them. The last, indeed, was not difficult, for the guest, a veteran *causeur*, knew better even than she did his *fort*, and seized the thread that led to it. It was only by inference, only by inquiring why it was that one talked more easily at her house than anywhere else, that one discovered the perfection of her art. The influence of women was then omnipotent: they gave reputation, they gave fashion, they even gave political power.'

'The influence of women,' said Rivet, 'is considerable now.'

'Yes,' said Tocqueville, ' but in a very different way. It is not the influence of mistresses, or of friends, but of wives. And generally it is mischievous. Its effect is to destroy political independence. This is a consequence of the poverty of our public men. The wife is always there suggesting how much a little expenditure here, and a little there, would add to the comfort of the *ménage*; and the husband barters his principles for a few thousands of francs.'

'The Limousin,' said Rivet, 'is among the least altered parts of France. I was at a wedding near Limoges two or three years ago, to honour which, for four days running, seventy to eighty neighbours came every day, and went away the next.'

'Where did they sleep?' I asked.

'Why, a great portion of them,' he answered, 'did not sleep at all. They danced, or talked, or amused themselves otherwise all night, and rode away in the morning. For those who chose to sleep, several rooms were strewed with mattresses as close as the floor could hold them, and there they lay, the men in one room, the women in another. Many of the ladies arrived on horseback followed by a donkey carrying the ball-dress in a band-box.'

'Among the things,' continued Tocqueville, 'which have disappeared with the *ancien régime*, are its habits of expenditure.[1] Nobody could now decently and comfortably spend above 200,000 francs a year; to waste more he must gamble or give into some absurdity. No expense has been more reduced than that of servants. The *femme de charge*—your housekeeper—scarcely exists. Nor is the *femme de chambre* in the capacity of your lady's maid commonly seen; the duties are usually divided among the other servants, and so are those of your housemaid. Then we pay much lower wages. I give Eugène 600 francs a year—but that is quite an exception. The general rate is from 400 to 500.

'Eugène,' he added, 'is a man whom I have always envied, and I envy him now. If happiness consists in the correspondence of our wishes to our powers, as I believe that it does, he must be happy. I have all my life

---

[1] It is evident that this was written before the Second Empire.—ED.

been striving at things, not one of which I shall completely obtain. In becoming a thoroughly good servant he has done all that he wishes to do; in getting a master and mistress to whom he is attached, and who are attached to him, he has obtained all that he wishes to obtain. To sum up all, he is a hero. He fought like a lion in June.'

We ended our walk by calling on the *curé*. He has a pretty little house and a good garden. They belong to the benefice. He surprised me by saying that the population of his parish averaged only three to the house. There are few servants and no lodgers. In many cases, therefore, a house is inhabited by a single person. There is something dreary in the idea; but it must be recollected that the house is very small, and the neighbour very near. He estimated the number of children to a marriage at three.

In the evening Rivet left us.

St. Lo, August 26, 1850.—To-morrow the Conseil Générale of the Département meets at St. Lo, and Tocqueville, much to his dislike, must attend. St. Lo was not much out of my way towards Havre, so I accompanied him. His horses took us half way, and we posted the remainder. The whole distance is eighteen lieues or forty-five miles. A lieue, the old demi-poste, being two miles and a half.

We talked of the changes in French literature during the last 150 years.

'If,' said Tocqueville, 'Bossuet or Pascal were to come to life, they would think us receding into semi-barbarism;

they would be unable to enter into the ideas of our fashionable writers; they would be disgusted with their style, and be puzzled even by their language.'

'What,' I asked, 'do you consider your Golden Age?'

'The latter part,' he answered, 'of the seventeenth century. Men wrote then solely for fame; and they addressed a public small and highly cultivated.

'French literature was young, the highest posts were vacant, and it was comparatively easy to be distinguished. Extravagance was not necessary to attract attention. Style then was the mere vehicle of thought. First of all to be perspicuous, and then being perspicuous, to be concise, was all they aimed at.

'In the eighteenth century competition had begun; it had become difficult to be original by matter, so men tried to strike by style; to clearness and brevity ornament was added; soberly and in good taste, but yet it betrayed labour and effort. The ornamental has now succeeded the grotesque; just as the severe style of our old Norman architecture gradually became florid, and ultimately flamboyant. If I were to give a Scriptural genealogy of our modern popular writers, I should say that Rousseau lived twenty years, and then begat Bernardin de St.-Pierre; that Bernardin de St.-Pierre lived twenty years, and then begat Chateaubriand; that Chateaubriand lived twenty years, and then begat Victor Hugo; and that Victor Hugo, being tempted of the Devil, is begetting every day.'

'Whose son,' I asked, 'is Lamartine?'

'Oh!' said Tocqueville, 'he is of a different breed—

his father, if he had one, is Chénier, but one might almost say that he is *ex se ipso natus*. When he entered the poetical world, all men's minds were heaving with the revolution. It had filled them with vague conceptions and undefined wishes, to which Lamartine, without making them distinct enough to show their emptiness or their inconsistency, gave something like form and colour. His "Méditations," especially the first part of them, found an accomplice in every reader; he seemed to express thoughts of which everyone was conscious, though no one before had embodied them in words.'

I said, that I feared that I should be unable to read them; and that, in fact, there was little French poetry that I could read.

'I have no doubt,' answered Tocqueville, 'that there is much poetry, and good poetry; that no one but a native can relish. There are parts of Shakespeare which you admire, and I have no doubt very justly, in which I cannot see any beauty.'

'Can you,' I said, 'read the "Henriade" or the "Pucelle"?'

'Not the "Henriade,"' he answered, 'nor can anybody else, nor do I much like to read the "Pucelle;" but it is a wonderful piece of workmanship. How Voltaire could have disgraced such exquisite language, poetry, and wit by such grossness is, inconceivable; but I can recollect when grave magistrates and statesmen knew it by heart. If you wish for pure specimens of Voltaire's wit and ease and command of language, look at his "Pièces diverses." As for his tragedies, I cannot read them. They are artificial; so indeed are Racine's, though he is the best writer of French that ever used the language. In Corneille there are passages really of the highest order. But it is our prose writers, not our poets, that are our glory, and them you can enjoy as well as I can.'

The whole road to St. Lo was English in everything but the houses. It ran between hedges, hedgerow trees, paths, gates, and even stiles—all of them things almost unknown in other parts of France. The churches, each with its tower and spire, put me in mind of those of our midland counties, but are finer. The finest is Charenton.

That of St. Lo is a cathedral, partly round and partly pointed. The form of the choir is irregular, the western side inclining outwards to admit a florid chapel. The aisles are divided from the centre only by pillars; and the tasteless moderns have run horrible painted wooden screens from the pillars to the wall in order to make a succession of chapels each with its altar, surrounded by a dwarf Grecian pediment propped on wooden pillars with gilt Corinthian capitals.

The position of the town is beautiful, on the side of a deep wooded valley; but as it rained all the evening and the next morning, I saw little of it.

The inn has a bad character, but I did not find it uncomfortable. I suspect that what I have heard, that even in the inferior inns of France the beds are good, is true.[1]

---

[1] Although M. de Tocqueville does not appear in the remainder of this journal, I am unwilling to omit it. M. Anisson Duperron has been dead

Caen, Monday, August 27.—Tocqueville took leave of me this morning, and I started, under a pouring rain, by the diligence for Bayeux. The country resembled that of yesterday, but was still more wooded.

The cathedral of Bayeux is, next to St. Ouen in Rouen, and St. Étienne in Caen, the finest building that I have seen in Normandy, far superior to the cathedral of Rouen; and I am not sure that I am not guilty of preferring it to St. Ouen. It has less lightness, but far more grandeur. The palladium or Wren-like central cupola is a solecism, but beautiful in itself.

From the cathedral I went to the tapestry. It is far better executed than I expected to find it. Many of the men and horses have great spirit. Harold and the other Saxons are distinguished by their moustache. The Normans are all clean shaved. The gentlemen generally carry a falcon on the right fist, apparently as a distinction. Harold does so on ship-board, Guy of Ponthieu when on his road to seize Harold, occasions on which the falcon must have been in the way.

The towns are indicated symbolically by towers not so high as a man, like those in the Assyrian bas-reliefs, which in fact the tapestry much resembles, though superior in composition and expression. The transport of the horses across the Channel seems to have been thought a great feat. Every boat is represented as full of them, and one compartment is dedicated to their

---

for some years. He was a deputy, much esteemed by the Orleanist party. His wife was sister to M. de Barante, the eminent writer, who died a short time ago.—ED.

landing. Each boat has a single sail, held by the sheet, not belayed.

In the battle, William's army seems to consist almost entirely of cavalry; the few infantry are archers. Harold's consists principally of foot, and they are chiefly armed with battle-axes.

In the last compartment Harold is falling from his horse, still retaining his sword, but the arrow which is said to have killed him does not appear. Neither party have visors: the faces of the Saxons are quite unprotected, those of some few of the Normans are defended by small nose-pieces. The horses are generally red or blue, which is intended, I suspect, to intimate the colours which we call red roan and blue roan, these being in Normandy the prevalent colours. I am inclined to think our word roan merely means Rouen. A roan horse is a Rouen horse.

I spent two hours in Bayeux, and then took a diligence to Caen. Caen is very large, and as my tendon has not yet recovered I saw it imperfectly. I visited only three of its churches: St. Sauveur, St. Pierre, and St. Étienne. St. Sauveur consists of two large chapels, very florid, separated by the widest arch that I ever saw in an interior.

St. Pierre has a wonderfully beautiful tower and spire. The tower, as is the case with several other towers in Caen, is pierced by tall lancet windows, with very deep receded mouldings. The vaulting, in the interior of the chapels which surround the choir, descends in pendent fringes resembling stalactites. The effect is not good. St. Etienne is the finest thing that I have seen in Normandy. The west front is plain, almost bald, but imposing from its height. As at first designed it was a vast wall, with a tower on each side, and a few round-headed windows merely to give light. The spires which add much to its effect, and indeed dignify the approach to Caen, are additions. What may be the merit of the rest of the exterior I do not know, for it is inaccessible to the eye as well as to the foot; being built up by houses on all sides, as is the misfortune of the greater part of the fine churches of France.

During the last two centuries, the walls and buttresses on which so much skill and taste and labour were lavished by their ancestors, seem to have been considered by the French as mere props for stalls, shops, and dwelling-houses Frequently, so frequently that I scarcely recollect an exception, one of the finest windows is plastered up to make a party wall. This is the case at St. Ouen, at St. Lo, at the Rouen cathedral, and at Bayeux. Many of our own cathedrals are thus smothered: the south side, for instance, of Westminster Abbey. A general cleansing of the cathedrals of France from these vile parasitical accretions would open a new architectural world. The interior is grand, almost awful. When one sees it, one does not wonder that the man who had the boldness and taste to plan, and the power to execute such a work, conquered the rude Saxons of England.˙ It is remarkable that the round and massive style of William the Conqueror's nave, and the pointed and lighter character of the choir, harmonise perfectly. They probably would not do so if the nave were light and the choir heavy, or if the two styles were mixed in the same parts of the building.

Tuesday, August 27.—I left Caen at eleven this morning by the steamer for Havre. To-day we had a hot sun, the first that I have felt in Normandy; there was no awning and I went below. After steaming for about an hour we suddenly stopped. Across the narrow channel of the Orne, down which we were running, two great sloops had thought fit to anchor; and they just filled it. For a long time they refused to move; at last they condescended to raise their anchors, and we towed them out of the way so as to pass between them, but in doing so got aground. This cost us an hour. We consequently did not get to Havre till twenty-five minutes to four. The train to Yvetot, which I had intended to take, starts at four. There would have been time to catch it, but for the formalities which throughout the Continent have been invented to consume time and trouble. The luggage was to be weighed, and that takes a quarter of an hour; it was to be put into a van, and that takes a quarter of an hour more. Then the office closes ten minutes before the train starts. So I was forced to wait for the next train, starting at half-past five. It was eight before I reached Yvetot, which is about three leagues from M. Anisson's château, St. Aubin.

It was a dark wet night. I got a cabriolet, of course without lamps, and we started at half-past eight. After we had driven half an hour, we saw dimly a huge object before us. It proved to be a hay-waggon, upset, and filling the middle of the road. The great highways of France, and we were on that from Havre to Rouen, are very wide, so we managed to grope our way round it.

Soon after a voice hailed us from the road. It came from a man who had dropped his purse, and he politely requested us to get out and help him to find it; a request, which my driver, I must say, not with equal politeness of language, rejected. We then turned off into a bye road, being, according to the driver, about a league from the château. We passed through a long wood, trusting to the instinct of our horse, for in the darkness under the trees we could not see his tail, much less anything of the road. Directly after we had emerged from the wood we heard voices, and found again the path blocked up. This time it was an over-turned corn-waggon, which completely filled it. The peasants who were employed about it, dragged our carriage up a slope into the field, and, when we had passed the waggon, dragged it down again. This was a rather dangerous manœuvre in the dark. They told us that we were a quarter of an hour from the château. We drove for a quarter of an hour, and for a quarter of an hour longer, and the path, as far as we could judge from its ruts and its stones, became worse and worse. It was difficult to suppose that it led to a gentleman's house. At length it seemed to end in a wood, and the driver admitted that we were lost. By this time, however, the moon had risen, though behind clouds, and it was a little lighter. The driver, who professed to know the road well by day, thought that he knew whereabouts the château lay, and we took a road which led in that direction. This part of Normandy is, *à la française*, all open field. If it had consisted, like the Tocqueville country, of inclosures and deep lanes, we must have resigned ourselves to pass the night where we were. The new path, however, ended in a ploughed field, and we turned back again. There was not a cottage to be seen, and I think that we should have wandered till daylight, if we had not met a labourer whom I pressed as a guide. He led us for above a mile across the field to the garden gate. Everybody but M. Anisson had gone to bed—the servant dressed himself and let us in, and M. Anisson was kind enough to come and drink tea with me. There is nobody in the château except M. and Madame Anisson, and their unmarried son and daughter.

Wednesday, August 28.—The château is large and has nothing military. It is built of brick and stone and belongs to the age of Louis XIII. It contains three stories; the rooms all look to the garden front, south-east; the other front contains only a corridor on each floor.

Early in the morning, bread and coffee are brought into the bedroom; at half past eleven there are short family prayers, at a quarter before twelve is the regular breakfast, and at seven dinner. The habits, in fact, of a century ago are continued; except that what then was called dinner is now called breakfast, and what they called supper is now called dinner. And except also, and it is an important exception, that they then prepared themselves for their twelve o'clock meal by full dress. Arthur Young, living in the country with the Rochefoucaulds, Liancourts, and other people of the highest fashion, bitterly laments having to put on silk stockings and to be *bien poudré* at noon. What is one fit for after that, he asks, but to gossip and play at cards? in fact these seem to have been their afternoon employments.

The great want in this country is water—not indeed from the sky, for Jupiter Pluvius is very liberal, but on the earth. Our supply depends wholly on the rain, which is carried off from the eaves by pipes meeting in one great filter of sand, and thence passes into two reservoirs in the cellars. Thence it is pumped or carried over the rest of the house—that for drinking is driven by a forcing pump through another filter, and comes out soft and clear. These cisterns are cleaned out once in two years. They are never recollected to have been empty, or even to have wanted water.

The peasants depend principally on ponds also filled by the rain. I asked if they drank such water, and was answered that nobody drinks water, except on very rare occasions or in coffee. Their constant beverage, and at all meals, is cider. The farmers and a few peasants have water-butts, filled from the roof.

As we were walking after breakfast this morning, a girl of about twenty-four, in a monastic dress, pale, with regular features and a sweet countenance and manner, met us, whom M. Anisson addressed as 'ma sœur.' She is the village schoolmistress. When he fixed himself here he found only one school for both boys and girls, kept by a man fitted for it neither by morals, nor knowledge, nor habits, but holding his appointment under the Minister of the Interior, and removable, if removable at all, only by legal proceedings. He resolved at least to rescue the girls from him; built a school-house and residence for a mistress, and obtained this girl from a neighbouring convent. Her mother lives near Dieppe in easy circumstances, her two sisters are well married, but she felt a vocation for conventual life, and obeyed it. She was going to call on Madame Anisson, but before we had finished our walk, she had finished her visit, for we found her at home in her school-house. She lives there alone on an income which M. Anisson calls nothing : a few sous a month from those among her scholars who are able and willing to pay, and what the Anissons give her : for she has nothing from her friends, and, as to the convent, she is not a dependent but a benefactress : out of her little pittance she saves something to carry to its funds. Every year all the nuns pass five or six weeks there *en retraite*, and she is going thither next week. The Anissons fear that she may never return, as she has an alarming cough and the worn look which often precedes consumption. Should she survive her mother she will have some fortune ; but in all probability she will renounce it in favour of her sisters, or give it to the convent—for though monastic vows are not enforced by law, they are scarcely ever abandoned. They are taken for five years, a longer engagement being illegal on the part of both maker and receiver, but constantly renewed. A nun who chose to quit her convent would be shunned and probably unable to marry tolerably.

The post brought in the death of Louis Philippe. The Anissons seemed a good deal affected by it. M. Anisson knew Louis Philippe intimately. He had a conversation with him at Twickenham in 1816, which has ever since dwelt in his memory. Louis Philippe spoke with regret of the reactionary course which Louis XVIII. was taking, of his abandoning the tricolor, and of his subserviency to the priesthood. 'And yet,' he said, 'he is a man of talent and a man of liberal opinions; but as soon as you put a crown on a man's head it seems to fall over his head like a bandage. I myself, who venture to blame and to criticise, if I were tried should perhaps commit, not perhaps the same faults, but others quite as serious. I see all this with great pain, yet I cannot venture to whisper my disapprobation. But those who think that I wish to supplant my cousin, and many honest and intelligent men think so, know me very little. The position of a constitutional king is without doubt a very fine one, but that of a Prince of Wales or a Duke of Orleans is much happier. I have rank, wealth, consideration, everything in short except power, and power I do not wish for.'

M. Anisson thinks that his prevailing passion was not vanity, or ambition, or avarice, but the desire to promote the interests of the Bourbon family. 'Of the younger branch?' I asked.

'No,' he replied; 'of the whole family.'

'Yet,' I said, 'he has injured that family perhaps irreparably. The great obstacle to the restoration of that family is the schism which his usurpation created.'

'He could not avoid it,' said Anisson; 'or rather, if he had avoided it, we should have had the Republic.'

'The theory at Tocqueville,' I answered, 'was that he might have saved the crown by accepting it temporarily as regent.'

'I do not believe,' said Anisson, 'that such a Government would have lasted a fortnight. The Republican party was then strong, far stronger in positive numbers than it is now, when its apparent strength arises from the number of factions into which its adversaries are divided. The doctrinaire party was angry and suspicious. Charles X. was known to have said that he would rather chop wood than be a constitutional king. The example of England, whose history seemed merely a type of ours, was present to their minds, and, perhaps without their knowing it, influenced their conduct. They forgot that it was the religious element which consolidated the throne of the successors of William III. If the Duc de Bordeaux had been a Protestant, and if the French had been a nation of fervent Catholics, Henri V. might have been a pretender as little dangerous as James III.; but it was absurd to think that the friends of monarchy would acquiesce in the substitution of merely an irregular for a regular inheritor. Believe it, however, they did, and no one more fully than Louis Philippe. He did not oppose the revolution of 1830, but he did not promote it. There is nothing of the conspirator in his character. He was guilty of profiting by the misfortunes of the elder branch, but he could not have averted them. For a time the reign of that branch was over. To attempt to prolong it in the forms which, from frequent and unhappy experience, we most detest—that of a minority and a regent—was perhaps impossible and certainly would have been fruitless.'

Thursday, August 29.—M. Anisson has bought a farm for 23,000 francs. It was deeply incumbered, and the vendors and incumbrancers were to meet him at Valmont, a village about ten miles off, this morning to receive the money and execute the conveyance. They would not accept cheques, so the money was sent to him by railway from Paris in a bag containing 20,000 francs in notes, and 3,000 in silver, and weighing therefore about forty pounds. We started with our bag at seven this morning. The road lay through an open table-land, slightly undulating, and apparently dotted by compact masses of forest. Each of these masses was, however, hollow. Each was what is called here a *cour de ferme*. Every farmhouse is surrounded by a rampart of earth about four feet high, called a fosse, and nine broad, on which a double, and sometimes a treble row of trees, generally beech, but sometimes mixed with oak, is planted very closely. It comprehends five or six acres, containing the farmhouse with its extensive out-buildings, farmyard, pond and garden, and a large orchard, where the cows graze under the apple trees. A similar enclosure surrounds every cluster of houses and every detached house. The object is to protect them from the sea winds which sweep over this high peninsula with tremendous violence. It gives to the country the appearance of a partially cleared forest; not a habitation is to be seen, nothing but open fields and lofty woods. The wind had shifted to the north with a bright sun. It was a fine December day: with all our clothing we could scarcely keep ourselves warm in the sun, and were frozen in the shade.

On our way we passed Trouville, a magnificent Louis XIII. château in a large wooded park. It was bought some years ago by a man who had made a fortune as a pedler, and passed his old age in a corner of the kitchen with scarcely a servant. Having no relations, he left it to his *homme d'affaires*, who has sold the park in lots and is at a loss what to do with the château. Valmont stands in a deep wooded valley which reaches the sea about three miles farther, at Fécamp, and is divided by a small clear river. We arrived at about half-past nine. The *notaire* told us that he had appointed ten o'clock for the meeting of the persons who were to sign, and that it would take a couple of hours to apportion the purchase-money among them and obtain their signatures; so that we had two hours and a half to visit the abbey and château. The abbey is placed just above the village, where the valley widens a little; a situation supplying for the monks their two great wants, shelter and water. It was founded soon after the Conquest, and was destroyed about once a century, sometimes in civil war and sometimes by the English, during the next 400 years. In the beginning of the sixteenth century it was rebuilt with great splendour; but seems not to have flourished. It had a lawsuit with a neighbouring community which lasted 300 years: it fell into bad repute and was suppressed by a decree of the Archbishop of Rouen, and the land and buildings sold a few years before the revolution of 1789. All that now remains is a part of the choir, and the whole of the Lady Chapel. The latter is elaborately beautiful. The roof is of the richest groining, the windows florid Gothic, painted in a masterly manner, with the legendary parts of the Virgin's history, her birth, education, marriage, and death. Over the altar is the Annunciation; the walls represent a room, with a bed on one side and a door on the other, in the middle is a table containing a sort of tambour frame in which is the Virgin's work, below is a little shelf of books. In front are two kneeling figures; one represents her, the other the angel.

The whole is of the delicate workmanship of the Renaissance. There is a bas-relief of our Saviour's baptism, and an alabaster tomb over which one of the Estoutevilles and his wife are recumbent, of equal merit. The *femme de charge*, who showed it to us, entered thoroughly into all its beauties.

M. Bournon, the present possessor, whose house is built on the site of the inhabited part of the monastery, and out of its materials, is an *avoué*.

The three businesses which with us are united in the

attorney, are in France divided between the *avoué*, the *homme d'affaires*, and the *notaire*. The *avoué* transacts the contentious part of an attorney's business: he is called in only to conduct a lawsuit. The *homme d'affaires* is the uncontentious attorney: he is the trouble-taker of the rich, and the adviser of the bourgeois. He manages purchases, investments, leases, and loans. This has been the most certain road to fortune during the last sixty years. The *notaire* prepares, authenticates, and preserves all legal instruments. He is both a conveyancer and a registrar. The number is limited, and the vacancies are filled up by the Minister of the Interior, but unless a notary is dismissed for fraud, he is allowed to recommend his successor—which of course enables him to sell his office. A *charge de notaire* in Paris may sometimes sell for 400,000 francs. When we consider the confidence which is reposed in these three persons, it is unfortunate that not one of them holds the position of a gentleman. An *avocat* ranks a little higher—he may become a gentleman when he has acquired high distinction; but then it is notwithstanding his profession: that scarcely ever leads to the bench.

From the abbey we went to the château, placed château-like on the brink of the table-land, and looking down on the abbey and village.

In this castle in the beginning of the sixteenth century was celebrated the marriage of François de Bourbon with the heiress of the Estoutevilles. Francis I. with his principal courtiers attended it. We were shown the apartment in which he is said to have spent some weeks:

it is the centre room of a tower with three cabinets, I suppose for his attendants, opening into it. The furniture professed to be unaltered. M. Anisson was incredulous. I thought it my duty to believe its authenticity; it certainly might have been collected from any broker's shop on the Quai Voltaire.

Of the old fortifications only a huge square tower and a part of the curtain leading to it remain. The modern part belongs to the times of Francis I. and Henry II.

The successor of the Estoutevilles and Bourbons is a cotton spinner of Rouen—a violent protectionist. At a public meeting a few years ago he attacked M. Anisson for his free-trade principles. Anisson had to reply, and is rather proud of having done so, before a Norman audience, with some success. It was in the spring of 1846. 'Look,' he said, 'at what England is doing; while you are clinging to prohibition, she is breaking all her fetters. Do you think that your industry, shackled by the legislation of centuries, will be a match in the markets of Europe and America for her young and untrammelled energy? Free trade must be encountered by free trade. Like the diamond, it can be acted on only by itself.' This illustration excited great applause.

This led M. Anisson to talk of his parliamentary life. He formerly represented as deputy the Puy de Dome, but after the revolution of 1830, his constituents required him to vote against an hereditary peerage; he refused, and was not re-elected. Soon afterwards the people of Yvetot sent to offer him a seat, which he accepted on the condition of being left at perfect liberty.

After the dissolution of 1843, he told Guizot that he was so utterly displeased with the turn which things were taking; he saw so little tendency in the Government to adopt liberal views, or in the Chamber to listen to them, that he had resolved to retire.

Guizot remonstrated and urged the certainty of his being re-elected.

'I know that,' said Anisson, 'as well as you do. I know that the man whom I shall recommend will be my successor; but I will not remain member of a Chamber, which, instead of advancing, is receding from all that I think right.'

Three years afterwards a peerage was pressed on him and he yielded.

But a seat in that house of peers was not a satisfactory position. It was indeed a good debating club: great questions were well discussed there, but it had no influence—and nothing could be more disagreeable than its judicial duties. It was almost degrading to have to unravel the turpitudes of Teste and Cubières.

I asked him if he thought that France retained the elements of an Hereditary Upper Chamber. He said, 'Yes. There are still many great fortunes in France, and the hereditary peerage gave the means of increasing them by marriage. In the chambers of a notary the current value of a peerage was 40,000 francs a year.'

At twelve we returned to the notary. The vendors were there, but there seemed little prospect of the termination of the business. Interest had to be calculated for days and even half days. There were no tables to assist them, and everyone challenged the notary's computations. I walked among woods as long as I thought it prudent, and then studied the Indicateur des chemins de fer, at the little inn. M. Anisson went backwards and forwards between the inn and the notary, reporting progress or rather the absence of progress. At length it was half-past five. He got desperate, signed himself, and left the money with the notary, to be divided among the claimants as quickly as their signatures could be got. The duty on the conveyance was 1,600, francs, the notary's fees on the part of the purchaser about 600 more. In all, nearly ten per cent., or nearly four years' income; for land does not give more than two and a half per cent. net. This is dear, however; the ordinary expense is estimated at eight per cent.

In the evening we talked of the separation of ranks in Paris. Madame Anisson maintained that distinction in society depended on personal qualities; that the only persons avoided were those who bored, and the only persons courted were those who amused. This Anisson stoutly denied.

'Do you think,' he said, 'that an amusing homme de lettres or politician is received like a Rochefoucauld? He is received, without doubt, with quite as much civility, perhaps with more attentions, for his host wishes to make him forget the distance between them, but it is a different sort of reception. It is not the reception of an equal. I am inclined to think that persons of different ranks met on more equal terms under the old *régime*.

There seems then to have been really a sort of fusion. There is none now.'

'How,' I asked, 'are the wives and daughters of your agreeable men received?'

'Oh,' said Madame Anisson, 'agreeable men have no wives or daughters.'

'That,' I replied, 'seems to settle the question.' I asked if power or place gave any advantage in society.

'Not the least,' said Madame Anisson. 'Great actions may, at least for a season—they make a lion. Changarnier was a lion last season.'

'What is Lamoricière?' I asked.

'Nothing,' said Madame Anisson: 'he is too *soldatesque* for us.'

Friday, August 30.—I walked with M. Anisson over the farm nearest to his house. It contains 120 hectares, or 300 acres, and is let on a twenty years' lease at 6,000 francs, the farmer paying all rates and taxes, which amount to nearly 2,000 francs more. This is a low rent, and was so fixed by M. Anisson in order to obtain a first-rate farmer.

This man's capital employed in the land exceeds 3,000*l.* He purchases a great deal of manure. The outbuildings are enormous. There are two vast barns, one capable of containing 20,000 sheaves of wheat, the other 25,000; for in this country, as in La Manche, there are no ricks. Each barn has its thrashing machine. The farmer's house is long and low, and contains, besides the kitchen, two sitting rooms, perfectly neat.

VOL. I. M

The stock is fine : a good riding horse costs 40*l.*, a good cow 14*l.*

Here, as in La Manche, agricultural distress is complained of, though not in the same degree; and the same explanation—low prices—is given of it. A fat beast scarcely sells for more than a lean one, so that little profit is made by the grazier. The labourers, however, who make, as with us, the bulk of the population, are better off than they ever were, for their wages have not fallen. The ordinary farm labourer receives about forty sous a day, or about ten shillings a week and his food, but does not dine with the farmer. I saw a long outbuilding near the stables, containing a table and some rude bedsteads full of straw: this is their refectory, and just now during the harvest the beds are occupied by men brought from a distance, but in general they are not lodged. Their cottages are seldom their own. The rent is from 50 to 100 francs a-year.

We went into several of them : they were neat, as well furnished as ours, and had small well-stocked gardens before them.

The lower and middle classes on this side of the Seine seem to be a hundred years more advanced in civilisation than in La Manche. The manners of this farmer and of another whom we met at Valmont were simple and easy; a contrast to the uncouth rusticity of most of those on the Tocqueville estate. We walked on to the little village of Tourville; it is quite as neat as the best English village. The houses are built either in alternate courses of brick and flint, or of narrow compartments of brick or flint in frames of timber. Each has its garden before it in excellent order. The church is pewed, as is generally the case in Normandy.

We talked of the careers open in France to a gentleman. From many of those which naturally suggest themselves to us he is almost excluded by the low estimation in which they are held. Such are the Church, the Bar, and Medicine. Unless under peculiar circumstances, a gentleman would not select one of these professions for his son.

France has not the Indian and Colonial empire in which the cadets of the English aristocracy find place. None but the sons of men engaged in banking, trade, or manufactures follow these pursuits. In time, agriculture, perhaps, will be a profession, but it is not so yet. Farming is in France, as it is in England, an expensive amusement. The great outlet is public employment, military or civil. The navy, however, is accessible to very few. The army affords a more considerable field : the road generally taken to it is to enter one of the government military schools—St. Cyr, Saumur, or the École Polytechnique, which are open to those who can pass their strict examinations, and give commissions to those who have passed through them, or to enrol, as is not unfrequently done, as simple soldiers. A still wider field is opened by the civil employments of the state, either administrative or judicial.

For either of these purposes, at about eighteen or nineteen, after he has passed through a college, a young man completes a *cours de droit* at the University of Paris, or of some provincial capital ; and then if he take the judicial career, after an examination which is not much more than formal, he is inserted on the roll of *Avocats*, and tries to obtain the place of *auditeur* in one of the courts ; thence he may rise to be *sous-procureur du Roi*, (or *de la République*) afterwards, *procureur*, and afterwards judge. If his son select the administrative line, the father tries to make him an *auditeur* in the *Conseil d'État*, which leads him, in time, to be a *sous-préfet*, and *préfet*, or to the higher posts in the public offices.

It must be recollected, however, that, as compared with England, the proportion of gentlemen in France, and indeed on the Continent, is comparatively small. The enormous number of persons whose fortunes enable them to refuse to place their sons in any professions but those which are held to be gentlemanlike, is peculiar in England. It is odd that we have not a word corresponding to *rentier*. We have the thing in greater abundance than any other nation in the world.

I asked what were the plans of his own sons.

'The eldest,' he answered, 'who is married, wishes for public life ; he will probably enter the Assembly at the next election. The plans of the second, who is twenty-one, are not yet decided ; he has passed the examination at St. Cyr, not with any military view, but as an incitement and a distinction. He is now going through some courses of physical studies in Paris. He sometimes thinks of diplomacy, but I rather discourage that as an idle life. He has time before him to choose.'

The young man is pleasing, intelligent, and well-informed, and so is the daughter.[1] She has the frankness and ease of an English girl who has lived in the world.

Saturday, August 31.—M. Anisson drove me to Caudebec. It is only in approaching the river that one discovers how high is the table-land on which St. Aubin is mounted. For three or four miles we were constantly descending. The view of the valley of the Seine from the lofty wooded bank overlooking Caudebec is magnificent.

Caudebec was the residence of Warwick when he was preparing the expedition against Edward IV. which terminated disastrously at Barnet. It was formerly a considerable town, the metropolis of its neighbourhood, and contains specimens of what were fine houses in their day, from the time of Henry IV. down to the Revolution. Now, from their unsuitableness to the habits of their present owners, they give it a decayed look. The church is a beautiful work of the sixteenth century. It consists of a nave, choir, and aisles, but no transept. In allusion to this want, Henry IV., who made Caudebec his head-quarters during the siege of Rouen, said that it was the finest *chapel* that he had ever seen. The painted glass is good and nearly perfect; only one window has been destroyed. At the bottom of one on the north, next the west door, a benefactress has introduced herself, followed by a line of daughters. The sleeves of her gown are open and at least a yard deep.

---

[1] Now the Comtesse de Bourke.—ED.

The key-stone of the roof of the Lady Chapel descends in what the French call a *cul de lampe* 13 feet. There is something bold in the appearance of this unsupported projection, but it suggests the idea of insecurity, and after all it is an architectural trick: it is really maintained by an internal bar of iron running down from the vaulting of the roof. The tower and spire, the arches over the doors, the pinnacles, indeed the whole exterior, are elaborately enriched with shrines, niches, statues, and all the gorgeousness of the most florid Gothic. We returned through the forest of Maulevrier, one of a set of national forests which extend widely over this part of Normandy. It is an unprofitable property. 'It has been ascertained,' said M. Anisson, 'that the treasury would gain if all the national forests were given away. We should get from the *impôt foncier* a larger income than they now afford, after deducting the expenses of management. But they are kept as a capital to be drawn upon in every revolution. In 1830 and again in 1848, the new Government found the sale of some square miles of forest a convenient resource; and we may often have to employ it again.'

We got out at St. Gertrude to look at the village church, desecrated in 1793 and restored during the last two or three years at the joint expense of the Government and of the parish: M. Anisson being the principal contributor. It was formerly rich in painted glass and in elaborate shrines and niches. The former has disappeared, a few of the latter remain and show great delicacy and beauty. The expense was 14,000 francs, of which the Government gave 7,000. These local subsidies form an important part of the budget.

The Government, however, in respect of its enormous land tax, is a joint proprietor, and cannot perhaps follow our example of rejecting such claims. When we had re-ascended the plateau on which St. Aubin stands it was like passing from summer to winter.

We talked of the country clergy. M. Anisson is less favourable to them than Tocqueville. He thinks very ill of their information, and not well, at least not universally well, of their morals. There are none whom he could invite to his house. He agrees with Tocqueville as to the great increase of religious feeling since the revolution of 1789, and his experience is long. He was educated in England, and returned to Paris, at the age of sixteen, on August 10, 1792. He came back because his absence in England was called an emigration, and endangered his father. His return, however, was useless. His father was guillotined, his mother would have shared the same fate if Robespierre's power had lasted a few days longer, for she had been examined by Fouquier Tinville, and the day of trial was fixed. He and his brother were in surveillance in a house a few miles from Paris. In the same house, in disguise, was Gillaume, an ex-member of the Constituent Assembly, who prepared what is called the petition of the 18,000, asking pardon for Louis XVI. He first introduced Anisson to the knowledge of the works of Adam Smith, and may thus have influenced his whole subsequent life. One day Anisson found Gillaume's pistols on the table:

they were out of order and he cleaned and loaded them. A few days after, Gillaume's retreat was discovered, and the *gardes municipaux* came to arrest him. He used the pistols, but it was to destroy himself.

Sunday, September 1.—We drove to Allonville, a village about three miles off, to see the great oak supposed to be more than 800 years old. Its diameter is 36 feet near the ground, and 26 feet at the height of a man. Two chapels are hollowed out of its trunk, one level with the earth, and bearing the date of 1696, the other half way up. Each is consecrated and from time to time used. Every aperture is carefully roofed, and thus protected, the oak may well last for some centuries more. Its bark seems healthy, and at about 20 feet from the ground it sends out lateral boughs which would be respectable trees. If its age be correctly estimated, it must have been a fine tree in the times of the Conqueror.

Close to it is the château of Bellefosse, surrounded by the usual hedge of tall trees, which in this instance are clipped up to about 50 feet high, like those in the Tuileries gardens, so as to form a vast wall of verdure. I thought the effect good. The Anissons objected to it as too formal. They do not seem to have any intercourse with the inhabitants of Bellefosse, or, indeed, with any of their other neighbours, if other neighbours they have. And this I find is generally the case in the country. While I was at Tocqueville, a gentleman and lady, living about five miles off, once dined with us, and there were two morning visits—which were treated as inflictions: these were all the neighbours that I saw during three weeks. Madame Anisson, who has lived in English country-houses in what are called good social neighbourhoods, wondered at our liking such a life. It was amusing, she said, to her as a foreigner, but she could conceive nothing more dull for the parties both active and passive, for those who spent a couple of hours coming and going, to sit full dressed two and a half hours at table and one in the drawing-room, or for those who had to receive them at six, dismiss them at half-past nine, and then sit for an hour and a half alone with nothing to do but to talk over their guests. We talked of the want, in English, of words answering to Monsieur, Madame, and Mademoiselle.

'What do you do,' said Madame Anisson, 'when you want to attract a person's attention?'

'You call to him,' I said, 'by his name.'

'But,' answered she, 'if you do not know his name, can you address anybody by the word "Mister" or "Mistress" or "Miss"?'

'No,' I said; 'if you do not know the name, you have nothing to do for it but to catch the eye.'

'With us,' she replied, 'the name is very seldom used, except, indeed, by royal personages. The Queen used to address me as Madame Anisson, to show that she knew my name, but in society it would be bad taste.'

I left St. Aubin on Monday, September 2nd, after breakfast, took the railway to Havre, and the boat in the evening, was at Southampton at nine the next morning, and at home by three in the afternoon.

I never made a pleasanter tour. I saw grand architecture, fine scenery, and agreeable and interesting society. And I never had so good an opportunity of recording my impressions. As we did not breakfast till half-past eleven, and I rose at half-past six and went out little before breakfast, I wrote every morning for about four hours.

But I found that only a very small part of a day's talk, and not the most amusing part, would bear to be recorded. Anecdotes, and serious discussions, may appear as well on paper as in reality, but the light play of easy conversation is as evanescent as the gestures of Mrs. Siddons or the tones of Fanny Kemble. In general, in the morning I could recollect all the outline, and most of the details of what had been said in the evening before—but scarcely ever could make use of either of them. The bulk of what I have preserved passed in morning walks or drives.

N. W. SENIOR.

CORRESPONDENCE.

Malvern, October 2, 1850.

My dear M. de Tocqueville,—By this time I presume that you are in Paris, or Versailles.

I had a pleasant day at Bayeux and Caen after I quitted you, then a very agreeable week with the Anissons, then another at Bowood (the inhabitants of which place are anxious to be most kindly remembered to you), and I have been now three weeks here trying the water cure.

My Normandy tour dwells in my recollection as the most agreeable three weeks I ever spent. I do not think that I ever saw so much or learned so much in so short a time. I have brought home a full journal, which I will bring to you at Paris; it is now under the copyist's hands. I hope that you will find me a not unfaithful Boswell.

I can tell you nothing of politics, having thought nothing of them since I left you; at least of the politics of the century. The politics of the seventeenth and eighteenth centuries have engaged my attention very closely, for I have been reviewing Lord Campbell's 'Lives of the Chief Justices,' and in the course of my labours have made myself a fair scholar in the affairs of the Stuarts and the Georges.

With our united kindest regards to you and to Madame de Tocqueville, believe me ever yours,

N. W. SENIOR.

Kensington, October 18, 1850.

My dear M. de Tocqueville,—Of course you have made us exceedingly happy.[1]

If Rome or Naples will do, perhaps we may not think it advisable to go farther; but of all this we will talk when we have the happiness of seeing you in Paris.

What is the day on which you start?

[1] M. and Madame de Tocqueville had agreed to meet us in Italy.—ED.

I hope that you will take with you something to write on.

We shall not leave Turin before the 9th or 10th of November, nor Genoa before the 12th or 13th.

I had not permission to copy Bugeaud's letter. Nor could I have supported the fatigue of doing so—nor had I time, for it was in my hands only two days. I could translate much faster than I could copy. But of course the original would have been far more interesting than my version. Perhaps the person to whom it was written may publish it.

It was not intended to be concealed.

Can you give us letters for Naples? Those for the Ambassador and Consul at Rome and Civita Vecchia will be valuable.

Pray write in the blank pages of the Journal. Your notes will be more valuable than the original.

Ever yours,
N. W. SENIOR.[1]

Florence, Monday, December 3, 1850.

My dear M. de Tocqueville,—We are grieved to hear of the inconveniences of the journey, and not surprised at Madame de Tocqueville's horror of the sea.

Till within the last hour we were determined to be at Naples, by the 'Lombardo,' next Saturday. But to-day there is a report that the Neapolitan Government has imposed a three days' quarantine. If that be so, we

---

[1] I omit several uninteresting notes written on the journey.—ED.

shall leave the boat at Civita Vecchia and post to Rome, and probably remain there a fortnight or so before we go on to Naples. Of course, if you are at Sorrento we shall pass some time there. My sister passed two winters or two summers there, I forget which, and was much pleased with it.

We must go for a time to Palermo; we have so many letters and so many promises.

The farther one gets from the great centres of civilisation, Paris and London, the more childish the people are.

The Genoese are inferior to the Turinese, and these people to the Genoese. I expect to find the Romans inferior to them, the Neapolitans to the Romans, and the Palermitans to all.

But they are very kind; the weather is charming; the works of art grand; and the rides and walks delightful. So we do not complain.

Kindest regards to Madame de Tocqueville.

Ever yours,

N. W. SENIOR.

Naples, Tuesday night, December 31, 1850.

My dear M. de Tocqueville,—I got your letter at about four this evening, on my return from Herculaneum and wrote a short answer directly, and tried to send it by the 'Santa Philomela;' but I could find no one near the New York Hotel who had heard of the 'Philomela,' or 'Antonio,' or the 'Sirene,' so I put it into the post.

I now answer it rather more at leisure.

We dine with the Hollands to-morrow and Thursday.

There are to be few persons on Thursday, for Del Carretto is coming, and he is not anxious for publicity. I wish you could come on Thursday morning, stay the night, and dine there.

If you come on Friday, by taking the 9.25 train you can be here by 10.45. So we shall in that case expect you at breakfast at 11. The Gladstones will come to meet you.

I have a bundle of letters from England, all disapproving Lord John's letter. Lord Ashburton tells me that everybody agrees that it has done no good to him or to his party.

The walls are scribbled over :—

No Popery.

No Bishops.

No Remission of Sins.

I do not understand the last disclaimer.

     Kindest regards. Ever yours,
         N. W. SENIOR.

TOCQUEVILLE DURING THE REPUBLIC.

SORRENTO AND PARIS.

1851.

SORRENTO.

JANUARY AND FEBRUARY, 1851.

CONVERSATIONS.

M. DE TOCQUEVILLE read this journal day by day as it was written, and made his corrections on the rough copy.

These are the conversations to which M. Ampère refers in his charming memoir of M. de Tocqueville published in the 'Correspondant.'[1]

'Nous faisions de longues promenades dans la mon-

---

[1] 'We used to take long walks over the mountains, for though so frail, he was a great walker. Sometimes we halted in some lovely spot, with the sea spread out before us, and the sky of Naples above us. We rested to take breath, and then resumed our conversations.

'His inexhaustible mind, which at no time displayed more activity or more freedom, touched, without undue haste or too rapid transition, but with even flow and infinite variety, one subject after another. They succeeded each other without effort, from the most important and logical discussions down to the most piquant anecdotes. Though always perfectly simple, he preserved, in the most intimate and familiar conversations, the purity of expression and admirable choice of words which was a part of his very nature. While sitting on the rocks around Sorrento I might have written down (and why did I not?) all that escaped his lips in those moments of friendly intercourse.'—ED.

tagne, car tout frêle qu'il était, il était grand marcheur. Nous nous arrêtions dans quelque bel endroit, ayant en face de nous la mer, et le ciel de Naples sur nos têtes. Alors, essoufflés, nous nous reposions quelques minutes, et les entretiens recommençaient.

'Son inépuisable esprit, qui n'était jamais plus actif et plus libre que dans ces moments-là, allait sans précipitation, sans secousse, mais avec un mouvement doux et varié, d'un sujet à un autre. Tous ces sujets se succédaient sans effort, depuis les considérations les plus hautes jusqu'aux remarques les plus ingénieuses, jusqu'aux anecdotes les plus piquants. Toujours d'un naturel parfait, il avait au sein de la plus grande familiarité un besoin d'élégance et de perfection dans le langage dont il ne pouvait se départir. Assis sur un rocher dans la montagne de Sorrente, on aurait pu écrire (*et que n'ai-je pas écrit?*) tout ce qui lui échappait dans l'abandon de l'amitié.'

Sorrento, Belvedere Guerracino, January 25.—We left Naples this morning for Sorrento, where we are lodged with the Tocquevilles and Ampère in the Belvedere Guerracino, an old palace about a quarter of a mile from the sea, and a mile and a half from Sorrento.

We have a glorious terrace and loggia looking north over the orange-covered piano of Sorrento to the sea.

In the pure air of Southern Italy we can almost count the houses in Naples eighteen miles off.

From Naples to Castellamare the road skirts the alluvial plain gained from the sea below Vesuvius, and derives its principal interest from the changing views of the mountain.

But from thence to Sorrento it is indescribably beautiful. It runs *en corniche* round the cliffs, which here sink abruptly into deep water. They are generally of a friable sandstone, like the Saxon Switzerland, and the torrents from the mountains have worn them into deep ravines, up one of which the road runs inwards, for at least a mile before its banks approach near enough to be united by a viaduct.

The view from the chapel where the road crosses a lofty promontory down on the table-land ending in the precipices washed by the sea, on which Sorrento stands, its white houses smothered in orange-groves, is as beautiful as it is singular.

We arrived early, and Tocqueville and I took a long walk among the orange-gardens up the hill.

He spoke with great regret of the Anti-Catholic movement in England.

'The Pope,' he said, 'was very silly when he divided England into dioceses and created English bishops. He threw discredit on his friends the Puseyites, and excited both fear and resentment by showing the extent of his influence, and the mode in which it is exercised. So far from increasing his powers of interference with you, he has much diminished them. He was most to be feared when he acted most silently. Instead of profiting by his false move, you have made one yourselves. Your burst of intolerance puts you in the wrong.

'The cause seems to be a bad one which is defended by mobbing priests, and breaking the windows of twenty chapels.

'I look to England as the great source and the great example of political wisdom and moderation. You have now set a miserable example of bigotry and violence, and your example in this matter, as has been the case in many others, is more likely to be followed where it is bad than where it is good.'

'So far,' I answered, 'as the present movement is directed against the Roman Catholic religion, I disapprove of it as much as you do. No Christian sect has a right to call on its Government to treat the doctrines of any other sect as erroneous. Each sect has its own doctors, martyrs, and tests; and there is no umpire to say which is right. Everyone who maintains the opinions peculiar to the Protestant, to the Roman Catholic, or to the Greek Church, has two thirds of the civilised world against him. But without assuming what Protestants have no right to assume, except among one another, that the Roman Catholic *Faith*, so far as it differs from our own, is wrong, it seems to me to be capable of proof, and to be in fact proved, that the Roman Catholic *practice* is in many respects mischievous. Generally speaking, a Protestant population is superior in vigour of thought and of conduct to a Roman Catholic one. On this ground I think, that whatever steps can be taken to repress growth of Roman Catholicism ought to be taken.'

'Not acquiescing fully,' replied Tocqueville, 'in your

censure of Roman Catholicism, or in the propriety of endeavouring to discourage it, it appears that you are taking bad means for that purpose. The inefficacy of persecution, whether by the mob or by the law, to repress religious opinions or practices, was supposed to be acknowledged.'

'Even if it were acknowledged,' I said, 'I do not think that it is true. Persecution may be impolitic and may be morally wrong ; but it is not always inefficacious. Witness Bohemia, which in 200 years was persecuted from Protestantism into Catholicism.'

'In the first place,' said Tocqueville, 'an efficacious persecution must be a ferocious one, such a one as you could not adopt; and secondly, I am inclined to think that Protestantism, mixing less with daily life than Catholicism, is more easily extirpated. You persecuted the Irish Catholics, and with some vigour, for a century and a half, and at the end of that time they bore a larger proportion to the Protestants than at the beginning. I do not believe that the meetings and protests which your Government seems to encourage, and the riots which it feebly discourages, or even the Acts of Parliament which it obscurely threatens, will arrest the progress of Catholicism, if such a progress there be. But they set a very bad example to Europe. The world was beginning to hope that toleration could co-exist with an Established Church and with strong religious feelings. It was beginning to hope that intelligence, morality, political freedom, and religious freedom grew together. What you are doing checks these hopes. It seems to show that the popular Government of an enlightened and moral people is even less tolerant than many Governments which you are accustomed to look down on. The precedent which you are setting will be a pretext for bigotry elsewhere.

'Observe, too, that the outbreak is not directed against what you call the practices of Roman Catholicism, but against its doctrines. Your archbishops and bishops in their address to the Queen do not object to the Roman Catholic Church because it requires the celibacy of the clergy, or because it denies the right of private judgment, but because it is repugnant to God's Word, and sanctions blasphemous fables and deceits.

'In other words, because it interprets certain portions of Scripture in a different way from yours.'

The Tocquevilles drank tea with us.[1]

Sunday, January 26.—Tocqueville and I took a fine walk over the hills. It had rained all night, and the sky was covered, but the temperature was charming, about 54°. The oranges are not quite ripe; the almonds are some in full bloom, others going off.

We passed a little chapel where Tocqueville always attends the sermon.

'Nothing,' he said, 'can be more amusing than the pantomime and vehemence of the preachers.

'I have often wondered,' he continued, 'that a nation which attaches so much importance as you do to religion, and which knows as well as you do the impotence of written speeches, should yet tolerate written sermons.

[1] The Tocquevilles and Ampère spent almost every evening with us while we were at Sorrento.—ED.

You will not let a man read in the House of Commons or to a jury, because you know that what is read is not attended to. You profess to consider the matters which relate to the next world infinitely more important than those which belong to this, and yet you treat them, and them only, in written discourses often not even composed by the man who delivers them.'

'You should recollect,' I answered, 'that the practices of all professions are regulated by the convenience of the professors: the practices of the Bar are arranged for the convenience of barristers; the regulations of the Army for the convenience of officers; the studies of our Universities for the convenience of the college tutors: so our ecclesiastical habits are arranged to suit the clergy. It is difficult to preach *extempore*. Some men could not do it at all, others would do it badly. Benefices are property: they are bought like other estates, and the duties are made such as any educated man can perform. If every clergyman were required to preach *extempore*, a man who has paid 5,000*l.* for a living might be forced to give it up.'

'That might account,' he replied, 'for the use of written sermons; but then how are we to account for the effects which this torpid, formal religious teaching seems to produce? How are we to reconcile the coldness, the worldly-mindedness, and the general want of enthusiasm in your clergy with the religious zeal of your laity? With us, the influence of the priest depends on his abstraction from the world, on his indifference to the ordinary pleasures, and his contempt for the ordinary pursuits of mankind. He tells us that this world is not a place of amusement but of trial; that happiness is not to be sought here, and if it could be obtained would not be worth a thought if it in the slightest degree interfered with our chances hereafter; that it is to our future fate which is to endure to all eternity, not to the few years that we have to pass here, that our attention and our efforts ought to be directed. But when the man who teaches all this is obviously thinking more of this world than of the next, when for one hour that he employs in providing for his eternal welfare he spends three or four in trying to obtain the comforts and enjoy the pleasures of this brief existence, it is difficult to believe him to be sincere.'

'Much,' I answered, 'perhaps depends on the absence from Protestantism of the ascetic element. According to the Roman Catholic doctrine the Deity is propitiated by human suffering. A man saves his soul by punishing his body. On that assumption, to enjoy pleasure is in the nature of sin, and to provide the means of enjoying it is sacrificing the next world to this.

'But we hold that a man may be happy both here and hereafter; at least, that his happiness here does not interfere with his prospects hereafter. And that a clergyman is not merely justified but bound to marry his daughters, and place out his sons, and leave his widow a comfortable annuity: this takes time and thought. A married clergyman cannot abstract himself from the world or despise the ordinary pursuits of mankind. If he were to do so he would ruin his family.

'He is necessarily a man of the world as well as a man of religion.'

'Still,' said Tocqueville, 'I do not understand how a clergy so occupied can excite the enthusiasm of their hearers. How, for instance, is it possible that one of your written sermons, read like a task without action or life or energy, can rouse the passions of the congregation? And yet roused they must be. Religious motives affect more the conduct of your people, religious ideas occupy a larger portion of their thoughts, than they do among us, where a much greater proportion of priests, whose whole hearts are devoted to the propagation and enforcement of their doctrines, who really act as they preach, who really show that they believe themselves striving for an eternal reward, are constantly working on the minds of their flocks with the popular eloquence of a Catholic pulpit and the powerful engine of confession.'

'One explanation,' I answered, 'is that our religion is, in a great measure, a religion of opposition. Much of it is expended in hatred or contempt of other persuasions.

'There is little controversial feeling among the continental Catholics. No attempts are made to convert them, they have no sects to divide them. They may think the belief and the practices of the Protestants imperfect, but can scarcely think them mischievous. Their religious feelings therefore, wanting the stimulus of opposition, require to be kept up by the constant, active intervention of the clergy. *We* live in an atmosphere of controversy. We have proselytizers all round us. No man in the higher classes is certain that his daughters may not turn Catholics, or his sons Puseyites; the lower and middle classes are assailed by the fifty different species of Dissenters; then the Roman Catholic religion, of which we are chiefly in dread, appears to us not only mistaken but destructive. You *pity* us, but we *fear* you. And it is comparatively easy to rouse and to keep up fear. Our priests too, belonging to the aristocracy, influence the humbler portion of their parishioners by their expenditure and by their charities, and the higher by their society. The celibacy of your clergy, by almost excluding gentlemen from the profession, prevents their having much familiar intercourse with the higher classes.'

'I have often doubted,' said Tocqueville, 'whether, if I were reforming the discipline of the Church, I would not allow priests to marry. One objection to their marriage with us, is the practice of confession. We should not like to have the secrets of so many families confided to married men. That, I suspect, is the reason why our lay authorities prevent a man who has been a priest, even if he choose to throw off his orders, from marrying. The *Maire* refuses to authenticate the marriage, and the Courts of Law refuse to compel him.'

'Have you ever,' I said, 'considered the loss which the world would have sustained if the Protestant clergy were unmarried? A third, perhaps a half, of our most distinguished men in England and Scotland have been the sons of clergymen. A clergyman has almost always

a family; he always gives them a liberal education; he
has generally something beyond his life income, but not
enough for his sons to live on. They uniformly refuse
to be tradesmen, and therefore are forced into literature
and the professions, and succeed in them better than
any other class.'

'That is good for the sons,' said Tocqueville, 'but
must give an immense harvest of old maids.'[1]

[1] The following letter, in answer to one from Archbishop Whately, is interesting, not only as a commentary on the preceding conversation, but as showing Mr. Senior's object in writing these journals:—

Letter from N. W. Senior to Archbishop Whately.

My dear Whately,—I have read over the Sorrento dialogue, which is open to much of your criticism; but you must recollect that in all these conversations my object is to record what my companions said, not what I said myself. My own words are introduced as sparingly as possible, merely to render intelligible what was said to me. My journals are therefore full of most extravagant opinions and statements, unopposed, indeed uncommented on by me—but certainly no more acquiesced in than what is reflected by a mirror is acquiesced in by the man who holds it.

On the other hand, I do not think that I represent Protestant ministers as worldly or interested, that is, beyond the average. I believe them to be, in general, neither better nor worse than other people.

What Roman Catholic priests may be I do not know from experience, for I never came across them. Tocqueville, in all his conversations, both in Sorrento and in Normandy, speaks well of them.

C. A—— and my Italian friends describe them as immoral and rapacious. I lean to the latter opinion, but on very imperfect data.

Again, I believe that in France, of which we were speaking, and among the higher classes of whom we were speaking, there is much less hostility to Protestants than there is with us towards Catholics. And for this reason, that among the higher classes the men are almost all indifferent to religion, or think the Protestants nearer to the truth than the Roman Catholics.

Those among my French male acquaintances who are Christians are very rarely Roman Catholics in real opinions. They approach much more nearly to Unitarians.

Our religious feelings are kept up by living in an atmosphere of

Wednesday, January 29.—I walked with Tocqueville and Ampère round the massive walls of Sorrento. It must have been impregnable before the use of gunpowder.

In this friable sandstone the torrents from the hills wear deep channels, which are easily scarped. Channels of this kind, thirty or forty feet broad, and perhaps 200 feet deep, nearly surround Sorrento on three sides; on the fourth it rises from precipices which run out into deep water, and it has the further protection of high and solid walls.

We had just heard the news of the vote of the Assembly of January 18, that it had no confidence in the present French Ministry.[1]

'The last time,' said Tocqueville, 'that a French Chamber agreed on such a vote was in June 1830. An ominous recollection; but in 1830 the 221 had the country at their back.

'It is difficult to say how far the country sympathises with the Assembly. It has done itself great harm by releasing Mauguin from legal custody. The tribunals controversy. The French have no fears of their children or relations being converted. I never recollect an instance of a French girl turning Protestant. All that they fear is their turning nuns. They are in general much more afraid of their own priests than of ours.

Ever yours,
N. W. SENIOR.

[1] The President was beginning to show his determination to exercise despotic power. He had succeeded in removing Changarnier from his position as Commander-in-chief, and the Ministers appointed on the 9th were supposed to be tools in the hands of their master. Baroche was Minister of the Interior, Fould of Finance, and Rouher of Justice.—ED.

are furious ; all privileges, particularly those assumed by collective bodies, are unpopular. The retention in its service of such a man as Yon, is another fault. Its disorderly debates and brutal interruptions excite disapprobation, almost contempt. The President, on the other hand, makes no undignified appearance in public. His immense patronage throws all France at his feet. The framers of the Constitution meant to render him merely the subordinate officer of the Assembly. Within the limits of the Constitution the Assembly was to be Sovereign. But they have given the President means of power and influence with which they, the Assembly, find it difficult to cope. And I agree with Thiers, that if, in the struggle, the Assembly yields, we have the Empire under another name. It is possible that he may make a compromise with them on the dotation question, give up his Ministers, and receive his three millions—which of course would be dishonourable to him. It is more probable that his Ministers will refuse to continue.

'To be censured by the Assembly, and treated by the President as mere clerks, is paying a high price for office.'

'It is unfortunate,' I said, 'that Louis Napoleon has learned so little in England.'

'He learned in England,' said Tocqueville, 'a good deal. He learned, for instance, the value of private enterprise and skill. He is less inclined than most of his Ministers to interpose in all great works the action of the Government. But he has not learned even the principles of Parliamentary Government. He is resolved not merely to be his own Prime Minister, but to be almost sole Minister. He will not even submit to be controlled in his Cabinet. Hence arises the anomaly that the leading men in the Assembly vote against the Ministry, and yet refuse to take office. They vote against the Ministry, because they fancy that they see in them the accomplices of an usurpation; they refuse to take office because they would incur responsibility without having free agency.'

'It seems to me,' I said, 'that the Assembly ought to have made its stand against the aristocratic pretensions of the President in November 1849, when, in defiance of the spirit of Parliamentary Government, he dismissed a Ministry which was supported by a strong majority. By not resenting that aggression, you invited others.'

'That is true,' he answered; 'but the Assembly was new, and the President was new. We were very anxious not to begin so early with a quarrel, and we, the retiring Ministry, used our utmost efforts to obtain for our successors a fair trial. But perhaps, as you say, we were wrong.'

'What is the next move,' I asked, 'if the Ministers remain?'

'There are two moves,' he answered, 'by which the Assembly might endeavour to coerce the President. The direct taxes, which form the bulk of the revenue, are, by the Constitution, only annual. It might refuse them, or it might pass laws directly aimed at his power. It might change, for instance, the constitution of the army. It might exclude the army from Paris; in fact, exercising despotically the whole power of legislation, on all points that are not determined by the Constitution, it might seriously embarrass or even arrest his administration.'

'Would not either of these courses,' I said, 'induce the public to take part with the President? Each of them would, in fact, be fighting the battle at the expense of the country. You want, I think, here the expedient of a dissolution. With us, if the King returns Ministers whom the House of Commons disapproves, it stops, or rather threatens to stop, the supplies; not as a party move, but as a means of forcing an appeal to the people. It is dissolved, and the ultimate umpire, the Nation, decides. If it sends back, as it did in 1835, a House with the same opinion as its predecessors, the Ministers must go. If it sends one, as it did in 1784, with a Ministerial majority, of course they remain. You seem to have no means of consulting the Nation, but must wait till the Assembly has sat through its term.'

'A dissolution,' he said, 'with us would be a revolution. The President, especially a Bonaparte, could not be left even for a few weeks unchecked by a countervailing force. Some years hence perhaps, if we have then popular institutions, our Chief Magistrate may be allowed the power given to your Sovereign, but not in our present state of transition.'

'But,' I said, 'if you refuse to pass laws and the President remains firm, what is to be the result?'

'If,' he answered, 'his conduct were such as to justify

our accusing him of an intention to subvert the Constitution, we might seize the whole power of the State and impeach him. And these seditious cries, these promotions of those who uttered them, these dismissals of those who refused to join in them, this removal of the Commander on whose skill and fidelity the Assembly relied for its protection, are strong indications of plans of usurpation.'

'They might be urged,' said Ampère, 'as implying a tendency; but the President may certainly keep within the limits of the law, and yet make legal Government, except through his own Ministers, impossible.'

'Was he wise,' I asked, 'in indulging in an expenditure which forces him to apply to the Chamber for a further allowance?'

'Very unwise,' answered Tocqueville. 'He ought to have lived within his income, as the richest private man in France, without assuming princely magnificence. He would have been more respected and really more powerful. I have told him so a hundred times. I have implored him to lay aside his extravagant retinue, and to discontinue his ostentatious fêtes. But his instincts are towards expense, and his immediate adherents, who are as bad advisers as it is possible, stimulate an extravagance by which they profit. He is always thinking of his uncle. And the expense of the Imperial Court is, of course, the part of the Empire most easily copied.'

'In what way,' I said, 'does he get rid of so much money?'

'A great deal of it,' said Tocqueville, 'goes in gifts to

old officers. Much of course in dinners and balls, but more still in what is called *coulage*—waste, carelessness.'

'Of course,' I said, 'he has gained something by this expenditure, though he may have lost more.'

'If,' answered Tocqueville, 'his object be to become a Sovereign, he may have forwarded it by accustoming people to see him surrounded by a state and splendour inconsistent with private life.

'But I do not believe that his extravagance has been the result of any deep political views. I fancy that his real motive has been the pleasure of spending money, of gratifying his immediate vanity, and the vanity of those around him.

'It is wonderful how many men of talent and ambition have sacrificed their comfort and even their independence to a taste for expense.

'All that is going on,' continued Tocqueville, 'fills me with uneasiness. I wish well to the President, and I wish well to the Assembly, and I see them trying to destroy one another. Among all the different courses which events may take, the one which has for some time appeared to me the least objectionable is the prolongation of Louis Napoleon's Presidency, and I am grieved to see him make it the most objectionable.'

'What,' I asked, 'will be the prophecy that I shall hear when I am in Paris next May? During the three last Mays it has been an insurrection, and twice it has come true.'

'The prophecy,' he answered, 'next May, will be a *coup d'état*. Some of your friends will tell you that in a week the Assembly will declare itself in danger, appoint a guard of 40,000 men under the command of one of its members, and use it to drag the President to Vincennes.

'Others will assure you that the news which you may expect every morning is, that during the night the Palais National has been occupied by the troops, that the walls are covered with placards declaring the Assembly dissolved, and that all the leading members of the majority are arrested or concealed. And I will not venture to predict that neither of these events or, at least, that no event similar to one of them, will occur. In the present state of feeling,' he continued, 'nothing could be easier than for the President to make himself a Constitutional King. It is the form of Government under which France has been most prosperous, it is the one which has the most friends and the most effective ones. If one of the Orleans Princes were President, we should slide into it almost unconsciously. But this is a *rôle* utterly repugnant to all Louis Napoleon's prejudices and tastes. He cannot bear to be controlled by an Assembly, to take his Ministers from its majority; to submit his conduct to its criticism. I am convinced that he had much rather remain President of the Republic, with a vague, undefined, and, as he thinks, independent power, than become a Constitutional King, acting under the advice of his Ministers, and with little real power of choosing them.

'Of course I do not mean to say that he is satisfied to be a mere President. What I affirm is merely that he prefers it to being a Constitutional King. What he would wish is to be a king like Henri IV., or one of your Tudor sovereigns.

'He would not object perhaps to a Senate, which might always pay him compliments, and sometimes give him advice; which might take on itself the details of legislation, and register and promulgate his decrees. But, like his uncle, he wishes to govern.

'The folly of clever men is wonderful.

'Almost all the leading members of the Constituent Assembly voted for him. Many were enthusiastic in his cause. They gave to it the solidity of a party. Two ideas governed them, and it is difficult to say which was the most absurd. One, that he was "Nul,"—that he had neither talent nor knowledge, and that therefore he could be easily led; the other, that if he were unmanageable he could be easily got rid of, at least at the end of his term, perhaps before. They thought that he would be a tool, and a tool that they could break. In opposing him, my friends had scarcely any supporters except the Montagne.

'Cavaignac afforded the only chance to the Republic. He is not a man of extensive views, but he is an honest man, and he prefers glory to power. His model would have been Washington.'

In the afternoon we had a visit from Don Raffaelle Petruzzi. It is a relic of the Spanish domination that, among the middle classes, Don and Donna are the usual titles. Don Raffaelle is a young man about twenty-five married to a lady who on her uncle's death will have 25,000 francs a year—in this country an enormous fortune, but in the meantime he has little except his salary as a receiver of taxes. He is to give us an hour of his company every day as *Parlatore*, for which we shall pay five carlines. It is not easy, however, to find subjects of conversation. He has little information and still less curiosity. He has never been to Amalfi, never to Pompeii, never to Capri ; I suspect not often to Naples. We talked to-day about the functionaries of the neighbourhood. The Judge of the Circulario of Sorrento, containing about 7,000 souls, has a salary of 20 ducats, or 3*l*. 5*s*. per calendar month, and may get about 40 ducats more in the course of the year in extra payments ; so that his whole income is about 45*l*. a year. That of the Judge of the Circulario of the Piano, containing about 10,000 souls, is 25 ducats a month, making with his extra income about 60*l*. a year. The salary of a Commissario di Polizia, his inferior officer, is at least double ; showing the comparative importance which the Government attaches to Justice and to Police. I treated the Constitution as existing though suspended. He denied its existence, and urged, as a proof of its abolition, the change in the oath taken by public functionaries. It was, 'I swear fidelity to the Constitutional King, Ferdinand II., and to the Statute.' It is now, 'I swear fidelity to the King Ferdinand II., and never to belong to any secret society.'

Madame de Tocqueville is not quite well. Tocqueville and Ampère drank tea with us.

We talked of the throngs of Americans in Italy and

France, and of the annoyance of many English at their being called English.

'So it is,' said Ampère, 'with us and the Belgians. A Belgian persecuted me all my journey by being taken for a Frenchman.

'My resource was always to allude to his country. "Vous autres Belges," I said, "do so and so." "Dans la Belgique on pense comme ça."'

Thursday, January 30.—We took a delightful walk, the ladies on donkeys, across the promontory. The wind is north, and it is said to have been the coldest day that has been felt this year. Yet the sides of the cliff were covered with crocuses, violets, and primroses, and we sat for half-an-hour among olives and myrtles, looking towards the Island of the Sirens, and the iron-bound coast of the Bay of Salerno.

As we were basking in the January sun, Ampère told us a characteristic anecdote of the revolution of 1830.

A legitimist, whose name he mentioned, who had signalised his zeal by a duel with General Foy, was in the garden of the Palais Royal looking on philosophically at the attack on the Château. A man near him fired several times ineffectually. 'I think,' said the legitimist, 'that I could teach you to manage your piece better.' He took it, showed his neighbour how to hold it, finished the lesson by firing and bringing down a Swiss, and then returned it.

The pupil, however, begged him to keep it. 'I am

sure,' he said, 'that you will employ it better than I.'
'Impossible,' answered the other; 'I am for Charles X.'

Friday, January 31.—We went—Tocqueville and the ladies on donkeys, and Ampère and I on foot—to the Deserto di Sta Agata, a convent supported by the French and now uninhabited.

It is situated on the summit of the mountain which ends in the promontory of Sorrento, and commands of course the two bays and Capri, separated by a narrow channel. We returned by the old Roman town of Massa, and thence by a road which winds through olive forests by the side of the mountain sinking and rising to cross the vast deep ravines which everywhere intersect the coast. The view of Sorrento from the summit of the last ridge which overlooks it, is one of the finest in this fine country.

Saturday, February 1.—Tocqueville, Ampère, and I started in a light carriage drawn, as they all are, by three little horses abreast, for Pæstum.

They took us, without stopping to bait, in four hours and a half to Salerno, about thirty miles, by Castellamare, Nocera, and La Cava.

The road after the first twelve miles is execrable as road, but beautiful in scenery. The least interesting part is that between Castellamare and Nocera; it passes through plantations of poplars, lopped and topped, serving as props of vines. Vineyards so treated may be pretty in summer, but are frightful in winter. Where they predominate, as they do in every flat country near Naples, they spread over it a cold, russet, brown colour.

On each side, however, are mountains, all the secondary eminences crowned with white convents and ruined castles. The descent from La Cava to Salerno contains about six miles of fine scenery—first running by the side of a savage gorge with a torrent roaring at the bottom, then as it reaches the mountain side over the sea, turning off towards Salerno on the left, while a mule-path on the right branches from it and runs *en corniche* along the cliffs through Vietri to Amalfi.

Salerno is a considerable town, with a fine range of houses a mile long rising from the sea. We went to the cathedral, said to have been built in the eleventh century. Before it is an open cloister, like that of St. Ambrogio at Milan, the arcades resting on columns stolen from ancient buildings without much consistency.

The outside, like most of the old Neapolitan churches, has been whitewashed and modernised. There are some remarkable mosaics covering the pulpit and apse, and the bishop's throne. Three ancient sarcophagi found, according to the sacristan, at Pæstum, are employed as tombs. The bas-reliefs on two of these relate to the history of Bacchus.

Two bishops, however, repose in them. The third, which is the base of a monument erected not a hundred years ago to an archbishop, represents the ' Rape of Proserpine.' Gregory VII., the great Pope Hildebrand, is buried here.

On a hill, almost a mountain, rising immediately above the town, is an extensive mediæval fortification.

Sunday, February 2.—We started at half-past six

for Pæstum, and got there at twenty minutes to eleven, having been detained nearly half an hour at the ferry.

The road was through a flat strip of coast between the mountains and the sea, thinly inhabited by a yellow unhealthy population, which flies in summer to the hills. Its other inhabitants are pigs, wild-looking horses, and wilder-looking buffaloes, having, as Ampère remarked, 'beaucoup de physiognomie,' and sheep guarded by dogs whom it would not be safe to encounter on foot.

The beauty of the temples is in proportion to their age. That of Ceres, with its single row of comparatively slender pillars, is merely elegant.

The Basilica is fine, and, if it did not stand close to the Temple of Neptune, would be very fine, but it looks almost poor by the side of its mighty neighbour.

The Temple of Neptune was, I suppose, inferior to many hundred Greek buildings which we have lost. Ampère says that it is inferior to the Parthenon. But it is the most striking temple that I have ever seen. Much probably is owing to its situation on a solitary plain with the sea on one side and mountains on every other. Much to the wonderfully beautiful colour, a yellowish-grey, which the stone has assumed. Much to the transparency of the air and the brightness of the sun, and the deep blue, almost black, colour of the sky on which its columns and pediments seem cut, and more than all these to its being perhaps the most ancient monument in Europe. A monument which was already venerable from its antiquity when Rome was a collection of hovels, and Paris and London were the hunting-grounds of savages.

But after allowing for all adventitious circumstances and associations, taking it as it was 2,500 years ago, when it stood fresh from the workman's hands in the midst of a crowded city, with no merits but those of its size, its proportions, and its form, it must, even then, have been superior to anything which we are now capable of erecting.

I never saw a building which showed so much the courage, the devotion, and the sincerity of its constructors, or, to speak more intelligibly, which shows so clearly that their determination was, at any sacrifice of labour, to raise a temple which even a God might think worthy to receive his image, and which might continue to be its abode as long as any of the works of man can endure. If this was one of the works of the Sybarites, they can scarcely have been a people of careless voluptuaries.

The spot where Mr. and Mrs. Hunt were murdered, almost twenty-five years ago, lies on the old road which passes by Eboli. They had slept at Eboli, and his servant had put out, on the table near the window, the contents of his dressing-case all mounted in silver. A girl belonging to the inn saw it and spread the report, that a Milor, carrying with him an enormous treasure, was going to Pæstum; eighteen men set out from Eboli to intercept the treasure. The Hunts had lunched as we did, in the temple, had sent on their servants before, and were returning in an open calèche, when they were stopped about a mile from Pæstum. They surrendered their money and watches, but the robbers kept asking for 'il tesoro.' It never occurred to Hunt that what they meant was the silver contents of the dressing-case, so he repeated that he had given up everything. They threatened to shoot him if he persisted in concealing 'il tesoro,' and he lost his temper and rashly answered, ' Birboni, non osate far fuoco sopra un Inglese.' This was an imputation which they would not bear; two men instantly fired—one ball mortally wounded Hunt, the other his wife, and the robbers having successfully repelled the imputation, fled to the mountains. The Neapolitan Government would have hushed up the matter, but the English and Russian Ministers insisted on its being seriously taken up. A shepherd-boy concealed in a thicket had seen the whole affair; seventeen out of the eighteen were identified by him, tried and executed, and the eighteenth confessed on his death-bed.

The Neapolitan roads seem now to be perfectly safe.

We left Pæstum at a quarter to one, and, passing Salerno, got to La Cava at seven ; having gone with the same horses fifty-two miles over bad roads, in two stages.

Sunday, February 2.—I wished to spend a long morning at La Cava, which is beautifully situated in the midst of an interesting country. But Tocqueville and Ampère wanted to write by the courier, so we returned to Sorrento to breakfast.

The best way to visit Pæstum is to go from Naples

by rail to Nocera, and then by a carriage to La Cava, sleep there, and the next day take a carriage from the Hôtel de Londres to Pæstum and back again. It is fifty-six miles, but may be done in a day with fresh horses, and the inn at La Cava is excellent, that at Salerno only tolerable.

La Cava is worth a few days' stay; the inn looks north, but has fireplaces.

Tuesday, February 4.— Ampère, Tocqueville, and I walked to a suppressed convent of Camaldoli on a mountain overlooking Meta. Thence down the mountain side into the plain, the finest walk that we have taken— four hours.

We talked of the difficulty of conjecturing the future Constitution of France.

'Every form of Government,' said Tocqueville, 'has been tried and discarded. Absolute monarchy, constitutional monarchy, oligarchy, and democracy. Perhaps the most important element in a mixed Government, aristocracy, has suffered the most.

'Wherever the French went they attacked its wealth and destroyed its privileges; and when the Sovereigns came back, the only part of our institutions which they retained were those which were opposed to the aristocracy. Even in England you assisted it with the Reform Act.'

'The Poor Law Amendment Act,' I answered, 'was a heavier blow to the aristocracy than the Reform Act. The Reform Act principally affected the aristocracy of wealth.

'It deprived mere money of its political power. The Poor Law Amendment Act dethroned the country gentlemen.

'It found the country justices each in his own circle the master of the property of the ratepayers, and of the incomes of the labourers. It left them either excluded from influence in the management of their own parishes, or forced to accept a seat in the Board of Guardians, and to debate and vote among shopkeepers and farmers.'

'Whatever,' said Tocqueville, 'be the destinies of France in other respects, one thing is certain—we must have a Poor Law. There is something not very unlike it now in the large towns.

'Probably in Paris as much is spent in charity as in London. At some periods of the year one-fourth of the population have received relief, but in the country there is nothing, and in the towns it is ill regulated.

'It is unfortunate that Thiers, who on most points has so practical a mind, should have taken so absurd a course upon this. His scheme is a large expenditure on public works, *ateliers nationaux*, over all France.'

'Is he,' said Ampère, 'likely to be converted?'

'I fear not,' said Tocqueville.

'There is one point, however, on which I have not been able to make up my mind. It is the great question as to the right to relief. Whether we should or should not say, that as a matter of law nobody shall starve. If we give this right we must of course make this relief disagreeable; we must separate families, make the workhouse a prison, and our charity repulsive.

'If we refuse the right we may give to it some of the attributes of real charity, and make it a bond between the poor and the rich. Then the evil effects of a Poor Law on the industry, frugality, and providence of the labourer are much increased by the certainty, that, whatever be his conduct, neither he nor his family can starve.'

'I am not sure,' I answered, 'that a large amount of charity, unaccompanied by the right to relief, and also unaccompanied by the restrictions by which that right ought to be impeded, would not be as injurious to industry and frugality as the right itself, to be exercised only on disagreeable conditions. Everyone would hope to get his share of the eleemosynary fund. And two great benefits would be lost. One is the security which millions enjoy who never exercise their right, but have always the satisfaction of possessing it. It is like a dwarf wall between a road and a precipice, which comforts a thousand travellers, not one of whom it actually saves from falling over.

'Another is the repression of mendicity. Where there is no right to relief, it seems cruel to order the poor to refrain from begging, or the rich to refrain from giving. When a London beggar tells me that he is starving, I disbelieve him, for I know that he has only to apply to the relieving officer; but if there was no right to relief, I should have to choose between making inquiries, which I have no time for, or giving to a man who in all probability is an impostor, or refusing a man who may perish for want of assistance.'

'Even the right to relief,' said Ampère, 'is not a perfect security. I am told one hundred persons die every year in London of want.'

'I have no doubt,' I answered, 'that one hundred persons die there every year directly from want, and many thousands from diseases produced by want. They are persons whom illness, or misfortune, or misconduct, has thrown out of employment, who live, far from all the educated classes, in the horrible lanes and courts which are to be found in every great town; whom pride, or prejudice, or aversion to the restraints of a workhouse has prevented from applying for public relief, and who, after selling all their little property, have been surprised by cold and hunger in their cellars and garrets.

'Death by starvation often comes on, at last, suddenly. I saw a good deal in 1848 of a Captain Herbert, who was Poor Law Inspector at Kenmare in Ireland during the famine. Every morning corpses were found under the hedges along the roads leading to the town. They were always emaciated, the stomachs generally flat, so that the backbone could be felt through them.

'Money was found in the pockets of almost all of them. These were the bodies of persons who were travelling to Kenmare in order to emigrate, begging their way and keeping their little fund untouched for the purposes of the voyage; until they fell down from weakness, or lay down from fatigue and died in the night.'

The convent consists of a church and some neat cottages in which the monks lived separately. As we left it, I said that 'the two things which I should feel the most disagreeable in Catholicism, are its asceticism and its confession. I should detest incurring any useless privation or pain, and when in the confessional, should be always hesitating between the humiliation of disclosure and the guilt of concealment. Roman Catholics are liable to one sin more than Protestants.'

'What you call,' answered Tocqueville, 'the asceticism of the Catholics was in its origin a reaction against the sensualities of Paganism. And the passions which prompt us to enjoyment are so strong that I do not regret that some degree of abstinence is inculcated by religion.'

'As for confession,' said Ampère, 'practically no humiliation is felt. After the longest confession both the penitent and the priest forget all that has been said, as soon as they quit the box. They meet the same evening in society without the least embarrassment.'

'After all,' continued Tocqueville, '*you* are not free from asceticism. What can be more ascetic than your Sunday? You think it your duty to give up on that day certain pleasures which in themselves you consider innocent. You do not think it wrong to go to a play on Saturday, but you think that it is meritorious to abstain from one on Sunday. You think that you please God by making to Him that little sacrifice on His peculiar day. What is this but asceticism, confined indeed to one day in the week, but still involving the principle that there is something wrong in enjoyment, something virtuous in mortification?'

'This is quite true,' I said; 'but it is not a doctrine or a practice prescribed by the Anglican Church. There is nothing in the Articles or in the Formularies of the Anglican Church which requires an observance of Sunday different from that required by the Romish Church. Our ascetic observance of Sunday is a remnant of Puritanism; it came in with the Puritans, and unhappily has not gone out with them.'

We expected in the evening letters and papers from France, but a continuance of easterly winds has delayed the packet, and none arrived.

Tocqueville is very uncomfortable. 'I voted,' he said, 'against Louis Napoleon partly for the very reason which induced the great majority to support him; because he is, or at least is called, a Bonaparte, and partly from my deep distrust of his character. But when we had him, I was anxious that we should keep on good terms with him. He is essentially Prince—the *rôle* of Washington would have no charm for him. He has believed for twenty years that it is his destiny to be the permanent ruler of France, and his rashness is equal to his confidence. Still I think that it would have been possible, for a time at least, to avoid a rupture, and I have done all in my power to avert one. In all my letters I have urged my friends to conciliate him. But, now that the conflict has come, I earnestly wish that the Assembly may get the better. If the President succeed, if his powers, already perhaps too large for a Representative Government, are prolonged and consolidated, he and his court will become the masters of France. The late debates have shown us, for the first time, a party calling itself the President's friends. They are endeavouring to form into a permanent party the minority of 286. That minority consisted originally of as many shades as the majority. There were those who wished merely to blame one portion of the conduct of the Ministers, there were those who did not intend even to blame, but merely to express regret. I trust that it will dissolve now that the accident which created it has passed. But if it does not, if it crystallises into a party, such a minority opposed to such a disunited majority will soon become the most powerful body in the Assembly.

'The people, too, are now in a state of mind in which, whatever be its follies or its usurpations, they will side with the Executive. They are thoroughly sick of revolutions, and would sacrifice the Constitution to avoid a contest.'

'It is lucky,' I said, 'that if your Constitution is in danger, it is not a more valuable one. If we were to lose ours, we should think our loss irreparable, but you could run up one as good as this in a few weeks.'

'The Constitution,' he answered, 'is detestable, but it gives us shelter. There is no saying what might happen in the interregnum. It is of some importance, too, to consider what is the character of the man who aspires to be our ruler. You think in England, I know, that he is essentially pacific. That he represents the party of order, and that it is safer to have to deal with him than with the Assembly. Just at present, while he is thinking only of the means of buying friends and crushing enemies, he is quiescent, but he has notions about the part which France ought to play in the affairs of Europe which might make him a very disagreeable, perhaps a very dangerous, member of the political world.'

'You say,' I replied, 'that you have endeavoured to avert the conflict. But how could it have been averted, at least by what conduct on the part of the Assembly? All the aggression, at least until the Assembly turned and stood at bay on the 18th of January, seems to have been on the part of the President.'

'So it must seem,' answered Tocqueville, 'to anyone looking on from a distance; but almost from the beginning the whole tone and attitude of the Assembly has been unfriendly.

'Thiers' report of the affairs of Rome wounded him deeply; not so much by the censure which it cast on our negotiations with the Pope, as by the omission of all reference to his letter to Ney;[1] a letter which he thinks a glorious piece of statesmanship, and considers, certainly with perfect truth, entirely his own doing. Then the Chamber was stingy about the dotation, gave him only a part of what he asked, and gave it ungraciously.

[1] A non-official letter addressed by the President to M. Edgar Ney, expressing his admiration of the conduct of the French troops, and his warm approval of the policy which led to the Roman expedition.—ED.

Again when a Permanent Committee was appointed during the adjournment, his friends were studiously excluded from it.

'It became well known that the *procès verbaux* of that Committee were unfavourable to him, and hints were frequently given that the time might come when some use would be made of them. Changarnier's popularity in the Assembly was apparently connected with his well-known enmity to the President. But it was still more in conversation that their dislike and jealousy showed themselves. He revenged himself by trying to tease and to irritate them.

'Baroche, his Minister, endeavoured to dismiss Yon, their Commissaire de Police; they were weak enough to support him. The creditor who arrested Mauguin was set on by the Elysée, and the Chamber was imprudent enough to assert that its members were privileged not to pay their debts.

'This declaration of want of confidence is the first open blow struck by the Assembly, as the dismissal of Changarnier was the first open blow struck by the President; but there has been a latent hostility between them for many months.'

Wednesday, February 5.—We went, the ladies on donkeys, to Meta and round by the side of the mountain.

We talked in the evening of the Constitution.

'The Committee,' said Tocqueville, 'which framed it, consisted chiefly of administrators and Republicans.

'The first wished to continue the existing system of centralisation, and, so far as this purpose required it, to arm the Executive with all the powers of royalty. The second wished to deprive the President of all the privileges and immunities of royalty, and to make him merely the first officer of the Assembly. I tried to persuade them that these objects were inconsistent, and that if they imposed on their Executive the duty, or even gave to it the power, of universal interference, the head of that Executive would be their master; but I could scarcely obtain a hearing. The first day of our meeting, Lamennais proposed to give some little independent action to the Communes; he was opposed by Marrast—left, I believe, in a minority of three—and the next day resigned. Beaumont and I made a stand for two Chambers, and were beaten after a couple of days' debate. These were almost the only discussions that took place. Cormenin, who was President of the Committee, took on himself the duty of preparing the draft, assisted by Vivien. He brought to us every morning some part finished, and scarcely any beyond verbal alterations were made. Cormenin was our Solon.

'One part, and one part only, is good. It is the tribunal for the trial of political offences. The *Conseils généraux* of the eighty-six departments each select, by lot, a member of the grand jury, and out of this grand jury of eighty-six persons, the jury that tries the cause is also taken by lot. A respectable tribunal is thus obtained free from local prejudices.

'One objection,' continued Tocqueville, 'has been made to the Constitution which it does not fully deserve. It is said to have authorised the President to become his own Prime Minister by declaring him responsible.

'It declares him responsible for attempts to subvert the Constitution. A responsibility which he would have incurred whether it had been expressed or not.

'Of his five immediate predecessors three were banished and one was beheaded. But the better opinion is, that by the Constitution, as it now stands, he is not responsible for the general policy of his Government. The Constitution directs a law to be framed determining the cases, other than the specified one of an attack on the prerogatives of the Assembly, in which the President and his Ministers are to incur personal responsibility. No such law has yet been passed. When passed it cannot be retro-active. He cannot, therefore, at present, incur any responsibility, except in the specified case of his interfering with the prerogatives of the Assembly. The Assembly without doubt ought to obey the Constitution, and to pass a law defining ministerial responsibility and directing its punishment. But if they extended it to the President, and declared him impeachable for general mal-administration, or for unwise administration, I think that their law in those respects would be unconstitutional and void.'

Thursday, February 6.—We went—three of us as usual on donkeys and two on foot—to the Cape of Sorrento, a singularly beautiful walk, running round the cliff.

The whole cape is covered with Roman remains ; some

of them are supposed to have been baths, others belong to a Temple of Neptune.

In the evening the papers arrived containing the list of the new French Ministry. It consists of a set of clerks, not members of the Assembly, but taken from the public offices.

The Minister for Foreign Affairs, for instance, is M. Brennier, a clerk in the Foreign Office, charged with its Finance, whose business it was to audit the accounts of the French Ministers in foreign Courts—intelligent, but a man who probably never read a despatch in his life. Not one of them except Royer, who is a lawyer, has any practice in public speaking.

The Constitution gives them the right to be present in the Assembly and to speak—a right, which of course they must submit to use, and of course the exhibition will be deplorable. This is an attempt to carry into practice the theory of the separation of the executive and legislative functions.

If the people submit to it—and Tocqueville is not sure that they will not—Parliamentary Government is at an end.

Friday, February 7, 1851.—Tocqueville, Ampère, and I, with an ass carrying our baggage, walked over the mountains to Scaricatori, a little landing-place on the Bay of Salerno, about six miles from Sorrento. It took us two hours, the last two miles being a steep rough staircase which the ass would not descend. Thence we took a boat with four rowers, which carried us in two hours and a half to Amalfi, passing close under a range of mountains from 3,000 to 4,000 feet high, ending precipitously in deep water. Every rocky promontory was crowned with one of the picturesque towers erected by Charles V. as a protection against the Barbary corsairs. They were called Martello Towers because they gave the alarm by a bell struck with a hammer—martello.

Our boatmen rowed standing like the Venetians, an exercise which brings all the limbs into play, and gives them fine erect figures. Living in a warmer climate than that of Venice, they do not cramp their muscles by clothes. While we were lunching on the beach at Scaricatori a boatman stood opposite to us, leaning on the high prow of his boat, who was one of the handsomest men that I ever saw. He had no clothes except a linen shirt, open almost to the waist, and linen drawers going half way down the thigh. But though this is the 7th of February, he seemed to want no more.

There was a strong land wind, so we hugged the shore, often passing between a steep headland and an insulated rock. Wherever the ground between the mountain tops and the sea is sufficiently inclined to give a foundation for houses, it is dotted over with large villages, or rather towns, in which the houses rise like steps, tier above tier, and to which the only access is by mule-paths, or from the sea by little coves cut out by the mountain torrents into the precipice.

The most considerable of these towns is Amalfi, once containing, together with Scala, Atrani, and Ravello, which are its suburbs, separated from it only by the sharp promontories which the mountain thrusts out into the sea, 500,000 inhabitants.

Scala now contains the ruins of 130 churches. At that time, that is to say, in the tenth and eleventh centuries, the Republic of Amalfi was one of the first, perhaps the first naval power in the world. It laid down the bases of Maritime Law; it founded the order of the Knights Hospitalers of St. John of Jerusalem, which afterwards became the order of Malta; it preserved for Europe the Pandects; it claims to have invented the compass.

Now its squalid houses line the shore for about a mile, and run up the two deep gorges, each containing a torrent, which are divided by the mountainous promontory, on the top of which are the vast ruins of the Castle of Pontone.

We went up the second gorge which divides Scala from Atrani and Ravello, and then climbed to the plateau on which stands the Cathedral of Ravello. It contains two pulpits with fine arabesque mosaics. In this cathedral Pope Adrian IV. in the twelfth century celebrated mass in the presence of 600 Ravello nobles of whom thirty-six were knights of the order of St. John. I doubt whether there are now 600 families in all Ravello.

Near the cathedral are the remains of a castellated palace, with a cloister in two stories of Moorish pillars and arches: probably the work of a Saracen garrison, with which Roger of Sicily occupied the town in the beginning of the twelfth century.

We slept at La Luna in Amalfi, an ancient convent converted into an inn; the cloister, the arcades of which rest on more than 100 dwarf pillars, is still perfect. We had good beds and clean rooms and tolerable food. Three tallow candles were given to us: when they burned low we asked for more, but none were in the house, and the shops being shut, none were to be bought. So we went to bed for want of light at ten. No fireplaces, but the rooms, looking south over the sea, were warm.

Amalfi is a charming winter residence, but must be stifling in the summer.

Saturday, February 8.—We visited before breakfast the cathedral. Before it is a broad portico, of which the arches rest on columns of different orders and proportions, evidently taken, as are the architraves over the doors, from ancient temples. Within are some good arabesques in mosaic, and some fine columns stolen like those without.

The inhabitants are the most shameless beggars that I have ever seen even in Italy. Old men and women and children are beggars everywhere south of the Alps, but in Amalfi, tall, stout, well-dressed young men ran from their work to implore *qualche cosa*.

We walked up the Amalfi gorge, till the path terminated in a paper-mill. Every projecting plateau is covered with ruins; some said to be Roman, which I doubt, but many belong to the eighth or ninth centuries. Half way up the mountain the house of Masaniello was pointed out to us.

I am sorry that we had not time to visit Scala. Amalfi in fact requires days: we gave it only an evening and a morning. It is beautifully situated, and is a striking exhibition of decayed power and wealth, but I did not find it so pre-eminently picturesque as I expected. Perhaps in summer when the vines and fig-trees are all green, it may be much more so than it is in winter.

We returned to Sorrento in three hours and three quarters. The safest way to visit Amalfi is to sleep at La Cava, and then go on foot or on a donkey, for there is no carriage road, along the coast path through Vietri, Maiori, and Minori, which takes about four hours and a half. It must be wonderfully beautiful.

The course which we took is the shortest and easiest in fine weather, but either rain or wind would have made it intolerable. Since I have been here however—indeed, since I left Sicily three weeks ago—we have had rain only twice, and then it ceased before noon.

This is, I suppose, the only country in Europe, calling itself civilised, in which a large and populous district has no carriage road to it or through it.

In the evening Tocqueville told us the story of Ben Ferrhat, an Arab chief, which was told to him in the chief's presence, over a bivouac fire in the desert.

The Duc d'Aumale was crossing the desert to the north of Algeria, at the head of a column consisting of one or two battalions of infantry, 500 French mounted Chasseurs d'Afrique, and 1,000 native cavalry led by Ben Ferrhat.

There was a want of water, and he went with all his

cavalry towards some wells on a plateau at some miles' distance. As they reached the foot of the plateau, about an hour after sunset, the advance guard rode back in great alarm, and reported that on the plateau they had discovered the Smala, or travelling town of Abd-el-Kader. It was known to contain at least 6,000 of his best troops.

The Duke said to retire was impossible, they should be discovered and pursued ; that the only thing to do was to attack it. This the Arab auxiliaries refused to do; they were sent back therefore to hasten up the infantry. Ben Ferrhat alone stood by his friends. The French rode up to the camp and dashed into it in one compact body.

The Arabs, surprised in their sleep, and ignorant what might be the number of the assailants, took to flight, leaving their women behind them. Among them was a very handsome girl, the daughter of Kharoubi, Abd-el-Kader's Prime Minister.

The Duc d'Aumale having performed one really heroic act, thought that he might go a little further, and, *more heroico*, bestowed the young lady on Ben Ferrhat. Kharoubi, her father, went to Algiers, submitted to the French authorities. and then required the Governor, Marshal Bugeaud, to restore to him his daughter. It was difficult to refuse. The French had solemnly promised to respect the Arab laws, according to which a girl cannot be married without her father's consent. And his consent to her marriage with Ben Ferrhat, Kharoubi declared that he never had given, and never would give.

On the other hand, Ben Ferrhat was a chief of importance, and had just performed a great service.

After much deliberation, Bugeaud resolved to obey the law, and sent an aide-de-camp to Ben Ferrhat's camp, forty-eight hours' ride from Algiers, to require him to surrender his wife. He was much attached to her, and she was pregnant : but he submitted : brought her to Algiers, delivered her to her father, and then retired, like Achilles, to sulk in his desert camp.

Kharoubi, however, did not keep faith with his new superiors. A treasonable correspondence between him and Abd-el-Kader was detected. Bugeaud offered him his life, if he would consent to the marriage. He hesitated for a day, but considering probably that his power of refusal would terminate with his life, at length submitted.

News was sent to Ben Ferrhat, who arrived two days after it reached him, having ridden for forty-eight hours without stopping ; and when Tocqueville saw him they were supposed to be a happy couple. 'He was,' said Tocqueville, 'perhaps the handsomest man I ever saw, set off by a magnificent and picturesque dress.' [1]

Sunday, February 9.—I walked before breakfast to the Cape.

---

[1] In 1855, in Algiers, I heard from M. de Fénélon the subsequent history of Ben Ferrhat's wife. She was fourteen at the time of her marriage in 1842, and therefore twenty-seven in 1855, an age at which an Arab female is an old woman. Ben Ferrhat is a rich man, the Ben-Aga of his tribe. As rich Mussulmans usually do, he has taken younger wives, so that the romance of the life of the first wife is over.—N. W. SENIOR.

Before the gate of Sorrento, as I went and as I returned, that is at nine and at ten, there was a busy market, in which pork, vegetables, fish, chestnuts, willow withes, crockery, wood, bread, old clothes, and all the abominations which Neapolitans sell in the streets, filled up the road. The wind was north-easterly, and cold; with us the sky was clouded, but Naples lay basking in the sunshine so distinct that it might be supposed to be five miles off instead of eighteen. About two, a thick cloud covered Vesuvius. It suddenly dispersed at three, leaving the mountain white with snow.

The papers brought us in the evening the meagre result of the 'interpellations' addressed to the new French Ministry on the the 25th.

'The Assembly,' said Tocqueville, 'has acted as a large heterogeneous body may be expected to act. It has made an attack and recoiled: shown its anger and perhaps its impotence. I have no fear that what may be called the liberties of France, such as they are, will be diminished. We have now enjoyed legal government for thirty-two years; and we shall retain it. But I fear that the monarchical element in our institutions will gain more strength, and that the representative body will be made weaker than has been the case with either of them since the Empire.

'As for the Assembly, the probability seems to be that until it is roused in May by the great question of the revision of the Constitution, it will sink into inactivity. It has indeed much to do if it chooses to employ itself.

There are the laws respecting mortgages to be almost remade. There is a poor-law to be invented. There are municipal institutions to be created. But I fear that after the excitement of this struggle, it will be disgusted by its ill success, be unable to act cordially with the President, or with Ministers whom it despises, and will fritter away the next two months on trifles, or in undignified disputes between the Royalist parties and the Montagne.'

'Will the revision of the Constitution,' I said, 'be a matter of earnest debate? I thought that everybody was agreed as to its necessity.'

'Everybody,' answered Tocqueville, 'is agreed as to the badness of the Constitution, and all sensible and all moderate men are anxious for its revision; not only will it be a matter vehemently debated, but I doubt whether the requisite majority, three-fourths, will be obtained. All the parties who fear that it will be altered in a manner unfavourable to themselves will oppose the revision.

'The Montagnards of course will oppose it; they know that the next Constitution will be less Republican than this is, and I am not sure what will be the conduct of either the Legitimists, the Orleanists, or the Imperialists if any of them should fear to be a loser.'

Monday, February 10.—We walked to the mountain over the Cape, and thence home by a sort of staircase cut or beaten out on the face of the precipice.

We talked of the great writers of the eighteenth

century. *Les Quatre* it was agreed were Voltaire, Montesquieu, Rousseau, and Buffon.

'Whom,' said Ampère to Tocqueville, 'do you put highest?'

'Voltaire,' answered Tocqueville. 'Nothing can exceed the clearness, the finesse, the gaiety, and yet the simplicity of his style. He had a right to answer, as he did, to a lady who talked to him about the beauty of his phrases, "Madame, je n'ai jamais fait une phrase de ma vie." Next, perhaps, as to style comes Buffon; sometimes indeed, a little on stilts (the reader easily believes, what we are told, that he never wrote except full dressed, and *bien poudré*), but brilliant, and flowing, and sometimes even poetical.'

'Montesquieu is a little artificial; and Rousseau, in his earlier works, indulged in long sentences, managed, it is true, with wonderful skill, but still giving to them a laboured air.

'It is on his "Confessions" that his fame will rest.'

Tuesday, February 11.—This is the third day of winter, that is, of a violent north-easterly wind, which, when you are exposed to it, renders a great coat necessary. When sheltered from it and in the sun, it is summer. We walked to the two ports of Meta. Meta seems to be a much more thriving place than Sorrento. The streets are clean, and we found no beggars. Like many other towns, however, in the Neapolitan dominions, it has the marks of decay.

We passed many houses that must once have been palaces, with escutcheons, most of them defaced, over the doors, and fine arcaded cortiles within; now tenanted by persons of the lower classes or just above them.

Ampère talked of the revolution of 1848.

'It quite took me in,' he said. 'I believed that power was at last in the hands of the people; that being biassed by no class interests, they would wish to use it for the benefit of all, and that the experience acquired in sixty years of revolution had at length taught them how to employ it. I made a speech to my pupils in the Collége de France, which had the most brilliant success. When I said "We reject demagogues but welcome democracy," there was a shout that might have been heard across the river.'

'Yes,' said Tocqueville. 'You dined with me on February 24; the events of the morning made me forget the engagement. I came home worn out by the struggle, and overwhelmed by the result, and almost choked with feelings which I had not been able to express. I found you radiant with delight. This was too much. I poured forth on you all my wrath and indignation. I abused you for a man of letters, who knew nothing about politics, and I warned you that whatever or whoever gained by what had happened, it would not be liberty, or the friends of liberty.'

'Well,' said Ampère, 'you were quite right, and since that time I have been afraid to trust myself on politics.'

Wednesday, February 12.—The wind is still north, but its violence is over. To-day there is scarcely a ripple on the sea, and it is too warm for a great coat. It is supposed that the last three days formed the winter of this year. Yesterday, however, was sharp enough to affect seriously M. Ampère; he went out without a great coat, caught cold, and to-day is in bed. We rode and walked to the Marina or Port of Serano, a village between the Piano of Sorrento and Vico. It contains an eminently picturesque martello tower, a little pier running out into the sea, and some houses with arcades and flat roofs in the irregular style of an Italian village; above them rises the mountain, its sides covered with yellow sandstone and sand dotted over with ancient olives. All these are the component parts of Stansfield's great picture in the dining-room at Bowood, though they are not arranged in the picture precisely as they are in nature. I suspect that Stansfield sketched separately the different parts of the Marina of Serano, and then united them in the manner which he thought best in a picture.

Thursday, February 13.—We walked and rode to the Camaldoli Convent, and returned by the eastern side of the mountain.

Tocqueville talked of the resemblance of the present state of affairs in France to that which existed under the Constitution of l'an III, or of 1795 before the *coup d'état* of the 18th fructidor.

'In each case,' said Tocqueville, 'the Constitution was made by a single Assembly which had succeeded to a Constitutional Monarchy, and had ruled despotically, comprehending in itself absolute legislative and absolute executive power; in each case an attempt was made to keep the powers separate—to have an executive totally deprived of legislative authority, not possessing even a *veto*, and a legislative body confined to the business of legislation. In the Constitution of 1795, the separation was complete, for members of the legislative body were excluded from all public functions. The present Constitution allows them to be Ministers.

'At this instant, however, when not a single Minister is a member of the Assembly, the practical result of each Constitution is the same; and even when the Ministers were taken from the Assembly, the number was so small, that more than 740 members had nothing to do but to make laws. Now, this is not enough to occupy them, and even if it were, an Assembly elected by the people, and believing itself to be the supreme power, cannot resist the temptation to take part in the actual government of the country.

'The least that it requires is that the government should be carried on by Ministers in whom it has confidence. But the supreme executive power has the same pretension. Not only the power but the duty of selecting the Ministers belongs to it. Under the Constitution of 1795, therefore, as under that of 1848, the choice of Ministers became a subject of quarrel between the executive and the legislative authorities.

'The Directory was in appearance far less formidable than our President is. It was a composite body and a fluctuating one. What was more important, it was nominated, not by the people, but by the legislature. And what was more important still, the Nation was against it. The Nation, at least that part of the Nation which possessed political power, was Royalist. Not perhaps Bourbonist, but, as it showed two years after the 18th fructidor, Monarchical. And yet the executive then trampled under foot the legislative, almost without a struggle. It did so simply because the army was on its side. The mobs of Marseilles and Paris and the army were the only democratic bodies in France.

'We had conquered Europe, under the cry of war against kings. Every soldier hoped that under democratic institutions he should become an officer, and almost every officer, for every officer was a *roturier*, dreaded that if the *ancien régime* was re-established he would lose all hope of advancement, perhaps even his commission. The army therefore sided with the democratic executive against the aristocratic or monarchical legislature. And it was irresistible; who can say that it would not be so now?

'Perhaps the best defence of a national guard is the enormous power of the army. It is seldom that a national guard can be relied on against a mob, but it is a great protection against the army, for the soldiers are not easily induced to fire on persons in uniform.'

Friday, February 14.—The winter seems to be over. Though there was a sharp frost this morning, it is warm in the sun, and there is the dazzling haze from the earth which we see only on a hot summer's day in England. It is about the temperature of our finest weather in the beginning of September.

The news of the President's demand of an additional civil list of 1,800,000 francs has just reached us. Tocqueville thinks it so hopeless, that it must have been made for the purpose of failing, in order to give him a further subject of complaint against the Assembly.

'As far as I can judge at this distance,' he added, 'both parties seem preparing for a decisive struggle. Each seems to be confident in its strength. There is not a man of any importance in the Assembly who has not joined the opposition. A majority so constituted can scarcely recede. On the other hand, the President thinks that the Nation is with him. If he were to attempt an 18th brumaire, I will not say that he would not succeed. His difficulties would begin with his first success.

'He has a quality fatal to permanent influence over men ;—a love of inferior company, I mean intellectually. He is shy—he has little conversation, no readiness, he cannot speak ; he feels, therefore, ill at ease with men of talent—this is one of the reasons why he hates popular bodies. He fears and dislikes orators. He surrounds himself, therefore, with puppets, who, as soon as he tries to use them, will break in his hands.'

Saturday, February 15.—I walked with Tocqueville to Massa and thence towards the Cape.

We talked of Talleyrand. I said that he appeared to me to have been very indiscreet—that nothing could be more indiscreet than his celebrated aphorism 'that language was given to man to disguise his thoughts.'

'I do not know,' answered Tocqueville, 'that he is to be called indiscreet, for indiscretion is the frankness of a man who does not know that he is laying bare what ought to be kept covered.

'Talleyrand knew perfectly well that he was talking imprudently, but he yielded to the temptation of a *bon mot*, a temptation which no Frenchman resists; and perhaps he was right in doing so—for the charms of his conversation were among the means of his success. It was principally through them that he captivated Bonaparte.'

'Had Bonaparte,' I asked, 'good taste in society?'

'Better,' answered Tocqueville, 'than in most other things. His feelings were all aristocratic. He liked people of birth and refinement. He never forgot that he was *gentilhomme* himself, and though there was something brusque in his general manner, he could be delightful when he chose.'

'The Empire,' I said, 'must have been an amusing time.'

'Not very much,' answered Tocqueville, 'for civilians. They were obscured by the military reputations, and military life passed away almost too rapidly to be amusing. I have heard of whole regiments which in a few years were killed three times over. It seems absurd to say so, but one gets accustomed to being killed. A short time before I left Paris, I was talking to an old friend, Rulhières, who passed through most of the campaigns of the *grande armée*. He told me that at Friedland his men stood motionless for two hours before a Russian battery;—the only sound heard was the voice of an officer, who, whenever a man was struck, cried,

"Emportez-le, et serrez vos rangs." Nothing but twenty years of war—that is to say, the traditional rules of conduct formed during twenty years of war—could enable men to exhibit this patient self-devotion. Our revolutionary armies were fanatically daring, but they had not this passive heroism. They would have dashed at the battery and have been blown to pieces.

'Rulhières,' he added, 'told me a characteristic story of a Russian. He was a man of high rank who had been sent to our head-quarters on a mission, and lived for some time on intimate terms with our staff, particularly with Rulhières. At the battle of Eylau Rulhières was taken prisoner. He caught the eye of his Russian friend who came to offer his services. "You can do me," he said, "an essential service. One of your Cossacks yonder has just seized my horse and cloak. I am dying of fatigue and cold. If you can get them for me, you may save my life." The Russian went to the Cossack, talked to him rather sharply, probably on the wickedness of robbing a prisoner, got possession of the horse and cloak, put on the one and mounted the other, and Rulhières never saw him again.'

Sunday, February 16.—Tocqueville, Ampère, and I spent a day at Pompeii. I think that I was more struck than the last time by the splendour and good taste of the public edifices, and by the smallness, not of the houses, for each of the considerable houses covers a large space, but of the private rooms: the largest tablinium or drawing-room, and the largest triclinium or dining-room, is about twenty feet square. It is clear that there were no balls or routs in Pompeii, and that the dinner-parties were small. In the male public bath is the bronze framework of a window consisting of four panes, each about 24 inches by 18. The Romans, therefore, had glass windows not differing much from ours. In one house newly discovered, the statues round a fountain remain as they were found. They appeared to me in very bad taste: dogs, ducks, and dolphins of marble like the ornaments in a Dutch tradesman's garden. Probably the house belonged to a Pompeiian grocer.

Monday, February 17.—I walked with Tocqueville and Ampère to Massa and round by the deserto di Sta Agatha. During the walk and in the evening we talked of the Roman expedition.

'Of its three motives,' I said, 'the maintenance of French influence in Italy, the restoration of the Pope, and the introduction or preservation in Rome of liberal institutions, only the second has been obtained.'

'The first,' said Tocqueville, 'cannot be said to have totally failed. It is true that we have not increased our popularity; the Roman people do not know, indeed nobody knows, the efforts that we have made in their behalf; they do not sufficiently feel that, if we had not interfered, Austria certainly would, and that Radetski would not, have carried on the siege, or used the victory, in quite the same spirit as Oudinot. But still we are there. Austria has it not all her own way. We have shown that we are able and willing to take a decisive part in Italian affairs. If we had refused the Pope's application, and the Austrians had brought him back, as they certainly would have done, they would have had a pretence to object to any interference on our part. Now as masters of Rome, we have at least a right to be heard. I am not bound, however, to defend the Roman expedition. It was no act of mine. When I entered the cabinet we were already at Civita Vecchia. All that I could do was to impress on Oudinot the necessity of so conducting the siege as to avoid injuring the property of the whole Christian world, the monuments of Rome. In this attempt we succeeded.'

'Yes,' said Ampère, 'almost the whole damage which the siege has done is the destruction of the trees and frescoes in the Borghese Gardens; and this was done not by us, but by the Republican Triumvirs out of pure spite to the prince, for it was totally useless.'

'This mode of conducting the siege,' continued Tocqueville, 'actually occasioned to us some loss of men, and much of time, and exposed us to dangers which make me tremble when I think of them. If the unhealthy season had arrived at its usual time, and found our army encamped on the banks of the Tiber, it would have been laid waste by fever. If Rome had resisted for three weeks longer, this calamity would certainly have overtaken us, and there is no saying what political ones might have followed.

'Now the mode in which we were proceeding; making no use of shells, and directing our attack only against the quarters where there was nothing valuable to injure, was so slow that the day before the town surrendered, our engineers estimated that it would hold out for twenty or twenty-one days longer. Happily the municipality, which the 20,000 foreign refugees had kept down by the terror of imprisonment, executions, and assassinations, took courage at last, and forced them to let us in; but it was a happiness that we had no right to expect. We owe it in fact principally to Ledru Rollin and his friends. The Roman garrison speculated on the assistance of the Parisian mob. When the failure of that silly insurrection showed that there was no hope from France, they lost heart, suffered the municipality to treat, and began to make their escape during the negotiation.

'The cardinals at Gaeta during the siege were always contrasting our slow proceedings with the vigour with which the Austrians reduced Bologna. They did not perhaps, in so many words, require us to bombard Rome, but to obey them and bring the siege to an end rapidly, that is what we must have done. And if any other of the Catholic Powers, Spain, or Naples, or Austria, had taken on itself the settling of the Roman affair, the town would have been reduced in a week by destroying perhaps a third of it.

'From the time that Oudinot entered Rome in July, till we were turned out of office at the end of October, the whole object of my correspondence with Corcelle was to induce the Pope to grant liberal institutions to his people. I considered this as the most important of the three objects of the expedition: as an object affecting not only our interests, but our honour; as an object without which the whole expedition was a lamentable failure.'

'As between you and the Pope,' I said, 'I suppose that you founded your right to make this demand on his having required your aid?'

'Certainly,' he answered. 'When a sovereign requests a friendly Power to send an army into his territories, not to resist a foreign enemy, but to put down a domestic insurrection, he contracts a tacit engagement with that Power to follow, at least to a considerable degree, its advice as to the use to be made of the victory. You occupied Sicily merely as auxiliaries, but you made the king give it a constitution.'

'And on what,' I asked, 'did you found your right as against the Roman Republic?'

'As against the Triumvirs,' he answered, 'on their being at the head of a horde of foreign ruffians driven into Rome by the disgust and indignation of all other countries—who were oppressors of the Roman people.

'As against the Roman people, on the ground that France is the first Catholic Power, that the spiritual authority of the Pope is essential to the welfare of the Catholic world, and that some degree of temporal power is necessary for the permanent exercise of his spiritual power. On these grounds what *appear* to be the domestic affairs of Rome, and *would* be its domestic affairs if the Pope was at Avignon, have always been a matter in which the rest of Europe, Protestant as well as Catholic, has thought itself justified in interfering.'

'And what,' I said, 'were the concessions which you required from the Pope?'

'They were five,' he answered.

'First. A renewed recognition of the general principle of liberty and security proclaimed by the Pope in his celebrated statute of the 17th March, 1848.

'Secondly. A new organisation of the Roman Courts of Justice.

'Thirdly. A Civil Code resembling the Code of Piedmont, or of Naples, which are in fact taken from the Code of Napoleon.

'Fourthly. Elective Municipal and National Councils. The Pope by his *motu proprio* of the 14th October, 1847, created a National Assembly called a "Consulta," which was authorised to advise, but not to legislate. We required one which should have deliberative power on matters of taxation.

'Fifthly. The secularisation of the public administration.

'Of these requisitions, the two last were of course the most material. *We* perhaps attached most importance to vesting in an elected body the powers of taxation, but as respects the feelings of the Roman people, the substitution of a lay for a clerical administration was the most urgent of all reforms. Their hatred against their ecclesiastical rulers is indescribable. It is such that the Pope can retain them only while his capital is occupied by foreign troops. The instant that we go, unless the Austrians take our place, there will be a new revolution which will sweep away every clerical functionary.'

'You did not seriously hope,' I replied, "to obtain all these demands.'

'I believe,' he answered, 'that when we made them,' many of them were hopeless,—though I thought it my duty to urge all of them as earnestly as if I expected to gain my point. But there was a time when they might at least have been promised, and perhaps ostensibly performed. That was when Pio Nono first asked our assistance. He had then quarrelled with Austria. Naples was democratic,—he was on bad terms with Piedmont, and applied only to us. Cavaignac was timid and refused; but, if we ought to have interfered at all, that was the time. When the Pope was at Gaeta surrounded by the Spanish, Neapolitan, and Bavarian ministers, when he had lost Rossi, when he had thrown himself into the hands of the cardinals, it was too late to prescribe terms to him. Corcelle could get nothing but general promises. When he asked for something specific, Cardinal Antonelli complained that he was interfering between the Pope and his subjects. With great exertion he was prevailed on to grant an amnesty; but it was subject to so many generic exceptions that it rather resembled a proscription. All who had sat in the Constituent Chamber, for example, were excepted. All who had taken advantage of any previous amnesty, even all who had assisted in the destruction of houses for purposes of defence. We could not stand this. We told the Pope plainly that no executions should take place in a town in which the French flag was flying, and we gave those who were excluded from the amnesty the means of reaching England or America.

'Every other request was met by a passive resistance. With so weak a man as Pio Nono the influence of those immediately about him is omnipotent. The cardinals, old, ignorant, timid and selfish, detest all change, and he does not venture to differ from them.

'When urged by Corcelle, he used to answer, "That neither threats nor entreaties would lead him to violate a scruple,—that he was as much Pope at Gaeta as at Rome, and that the French might do as they liked."

'We were more than once in danger of his throwing Rome on our hands. He wanted at one time to go to Lorretto. Corcelle remarked that as our Lady of Lorretto was at that time under the protection of Austrian bayonets, such a journey would be unpopular at Rome. But he was met by a statement of the Pope's special veneration for that Virgin. What could one answer to such arguments? It was like a contest with a woman.

'He felt deeply his want of power to act for himself. He seems to have thought seriously of trying to obtain some administrators from France, and he bitterly lamented the loss of Rossi. He said to Corcelle, "C'est le seul homme d'état capable de soutenir une nouvelle politique que j'ai pu trouver, et on me l'a tué."

'His religious prejudices, too, are very sensitive. When Corcelle talked to him of legislative reforms, and suggested the institutions of France as a good model, he asked with an expression of alarm, whether we had not legalized divorce?

'It was a great misfortune to Rome, to us, and indeed to the Pope himself, that he did not execute his original intention of taking refuge in France. The scheme was, that the Duc d'Harcourt, our Minister in Rome, should arrange the means of taking him to France, and that the Bavarian Minister should carry him to Gaeta, where he was to embark. So Harcourt with all the Pope's baggage went to Civita Vecchia, the same night that the Pope went to Gaeta. Harcourt found the "Vauban" at Civita Vecchia, and came round with her to Gaeta. By that time the Pope had been two days in Gaeta, had been received with all sorts of honours and veneration, and found himself so comfortable that he refused to move farther. Harcourt ought to have foreseen this, and have taken the Pope instead of his trunks to Civita Vecchia.

'The whole influence of Naples was of course unfavourable to us, and it was exercised in the teasing, childish manner which was to be expected from her.

'When Corcelle reached Gaeta, carrying the first intelligence of our entry into Rome, and eager to make an impression on the Pope while his heart was expanded by good news, he was put into quarantine, on the pretext that the "Cerbère" which brought him came from Toulon, and that there was cholera in Paris.

'He protested; the Ministers could not venture to decide. The King was consulted; he asked for further explanations, and after a long delay Corcelle was permitted to land; but his papers and his secretary were detained on board the "Cerbère" in quarantine, and it was only the following evening that the King was induced to connive at Corcelle's going thither by night and stealing them.'

'How did the Austrians behave?' I asked.

'Better,' he answered, 'than could have been expected. Austria was then professing to be constitutional, and affecting liberality. Esterhazy, who represented Austria at Gaeta, thoroughly approved, at least in his conversations with Corcelle, the secularisation of the Government, and the power of the Consulta in matters of taxation.

'It is remarkable that one of the grounds on which the President dismissed us was our not obtaining greater concessions from the Pope; but directly we were gone, he himself, or at least his Ministers, gave up everything. His vanity was satisfied with having insulted the Pope by his letter to Ney, and with having insulted the Chamber by turning out a Ministry without consulting it, and his interest in the affairs of Rome was then over.'

'But what,' I asked, 'could you have done if you had remained, and the Pope had continued obstinate?'

'We could have set ourselves,' answered Tocqueville, 'right with Europe, and have refused to sanction by our presence what we could not prevent.

'Our intention was, in that event, to draw up a protest stating all that we had asked on behalf of the Roman people—the grounds on which we had asked it, and the manner in which it had been refused or eluded. To present it to the Pope, to publish it in the "Moniteur," and to withdraw our troops from Rome, leaving this appeal to Europe and to posterity. This was the threat which we found most effective with the Pope. In the full consciousness of his unassailable spiritual power he was indifferent to the manner in which we might think fit to deal with his temporal authority, provided we did not ask for his concurrence. But he dreaded being brought to the bar of public opinion. Another menace, which from time to time we threw out, though with less sincerity, for I doubt whether we should have ventured to put it in force, was a Congress on the affairs of Rome. A Congress to which, as was the case in 1831, the Protestant Powers with Catholic subjects must have been admitted.

'This alarmed him, but I suspect that he saw that it would be nearly as disagreeable to us as to himself.'

Tuesday, February 18.—Tocqueville suffered yesterday from the sun, and Ampère has not recovered his strength; so to-day we walked in the shade through the Sorrentine lanes. In the middle of the town is an Egyptian kneeling figure of black marble. Ampère read the inscription. It appears to have been made in the reign of Sethos, the father of Sesostris or Rhameses the Second, the greatest king of the great eighteenth dynasty. It belongs, therefore, to the most brilliant period of Egyptian art and power, about 900 years before the foundation of Rome.

'We wonder,' said Ampère, 'at the magnificence of Imperial Rome; at the vastness of its theatres, and temples, and palaces, and its forums, one succeeding another. But all this was merely elegant and pretty compared to Thebes at the time when that statue was carved. Thebes covered a larger space than Rome in its greatest days. The temples and palaces of Thebes were grander in their size and in their proportions. The Coliseum itself is far less impressive than the great temple of Carnac, with its 160 columns each sixty feet high.'

Wednesday, February 19.—The wind has turned to the south-east, and is damp. We wandered along the ravines of the Piano, looking into deep winding gorges, covered, wherever there is soil enough to receive a root, with oranges and olives. We talked of the Russian army.

'It is the only continental army,' said Tocqueville, 'for which our soldiers have any respect. They do not believe that the Germans, and of course, still less the Italians or the Spaniards, would have any chance against them with equal, or nearly equal numbers; but they dread the Russians. Excepting at Austerlitz, and then the Russians were commanded by Alexander, they have never suffered a complete defeat.

'At Eylau, at Friedland, at Borodino they were beaten—that is to say, they had to quit the field of battle, but their material force was not seriously injured, and their courage and discipline were untouched.

'Lamoricière, who is an excellent judge, returned from Petersburg in 1849, full of admiration. The officers are ignorant, and not always well affected, but the men have almost all the qualities that can be wished for; they can live on almost nothing, bear any fatigue and privation, have a mixture of love and adoration for their Emperor, glory in being Russians and soldiers, and as they are soldiers for life, are perfectly drilled and disciplined.

'He was present at a great religious ceremony at Warsaw. Before the altar was the Emperor kneeling with the appearance of fervid devotion. Round him was a staff of generals and *aides-de-camp*, whispering and joking, for the Russian higher classes have taken up infidelity since we have left it off. But beyond these were the troops gazing on the altar and on the Emperor, with apparently equal reverence.'

Thursday, February 20.—It was hot in the sun before breakfast, but towards noon clouded over, and in the evening some rain fell; the first since the day after our arrival, nearly a month ago.

We talked in the evening of the Memoirs of Louis XVIII. I said that they had deceived Lord Granville, who told me in 1832 that he thought them authentic.

'They were written,' said Tocqueville, 'by some one who had excellent information: those memoirs, and those of *un homme d'état*, and the Mémorial de Ste. Hélène are to be separated from the ordinary manufactures, such as those of Madame du Barry, Fouché, &c., &c.

'Who wrote,' I said, 'the Mémorial de Ste. Hélène?'

'An abbé de Château vieux,' said Tocqueville, 'who kept the secret, except to one or two intimate friends, during his life, but revealed it by his will. He wrote nothing else very remarkable, and was not even a Parisian, which accounts for his never having been suspected.'

From the Memoirs of Louis XVIII. we passed to the man.

'He was,' said Tocqueville, 'the only sovereign of France who has had the good sense, or the patience to govern constitutionally. He made a few mistakes at the beginning—offended the army by his *gardes du corps*, and still more by Ney's execution; but during the remainder of his reign he took his Ministers from the majority, and his policy from his Ministers, and reigned in as Parliamentary a manner as if he had been King of England.

'It has been said that the Bourbons are a worn-out race, and Louis XVI., Ferdinand I. of Naples, and Charles IV. of Spain are used as examples: but what can be more thoroughly Bourbon than Louis Philippe's family—the children of a French Bourbon by a Neapolitan Bourbon? And yet they would be a most distinguished family in private life. I cannot but believe that the French Bourbons are still destined to act a great part, and their present fortunes are preparing them for it.'

We left Sorrento on the next day for Rome.

CORRESPONDENCE.

Rome, March 1, 1851.

My dear M. de Tocqueville,—I impressed on Lady Holland's mind your ineffectual attempt to see her when you were last in Naples, and she hopes that next time you come you will let her know beforehand, and they will keep themselves disengaged for you.

We are splendidly lodged here, in the only set of apartments we could find in Rome, and find the hotel pre-eminent in excellence. From our rooms we see nothing but gardens, and do not hear a single sound except our own voices. The cooking and attendance are perfect.

I could hear no English news in Naples, but I found here a letter from Lord Lansdowne, dated February 17. 'You have escaped,' he says, 'a religious storm which rages with a fury that can scarcely be said to abate. It might have been avoided altogether, had nothing been desired but an improved organisation for the spiritual objects of the R. C. priesthood, and the mode of effecting it chosen with some knowledge of the temper of the people here, the great bulk of whom are more Protestant than ever in feeling, and have had this feeling wounded at every point that was most susceptible. Still with the exception of a few contemptible instances, the whole discussion has been carried on in a far more tolerant tone than would have been the case half a century ago.'

All the world here is mad with the Carnival, therefore I have delivered no letters, and seen nobody.

Kindest regards from us all to you and Madame de Tocqueville, and tell M. Ampère that we are anxiously looking out for him.

Ever yours,
N. W. SENIOR.

I have just seen M. de Rayneval—very kind and very pleasing. Many inquiries after you.

Sorrento, March 31, 1851.

My dear Mr. Senior,—Ampère has of course told you that we have been, to our great regret, obliged to give up our visit to Rome. He, no doubt, has explained the reasons which have forced upon us this decision. They are all connected with the health of Madame de Tocqueville.

Some excursions which I persuaded her to take after your departure have proved to me that she could scarcely endure the fatigue of the long land journey, or to do justice to the sights of Rome. I was afraid that her health might become as disordered as it was last year, and that we might be kept for a long while away from our country, at a time when it is so esnecsary for me to return thither.

Having well weighed all these considerations, we have made up our minds and are going straight back to France by sea. Of all sorts of travelling it is the one which I dislike most, but under the circumstances it is the safest.

We probably shall start on the 4th or the 14th of April, and in either case if we meet with no accidents shall be in Paris before the 1st of May. The certainty of often seeing you there consoles us for not being able to join you, as we intended, in Rome.

As far as I know there is no news in Sorrento, and as for what is happening in the rest of the world, especially in France, I know no longer anything at all about it. When one has been absent from that country for more than five months one must give up forming any judgment or speaking about it. The study must begin over again.

Don Gaetano continues to make little figures like those which we admired together, and Don Raffaelle continues to gape in our faces. This is all the intelligence which I can collect for you, for I think that I have caught the prevailing malady of the country, and that I am beginning to be as much without ideas as are all the inhabitants.

Remember us particularly to your ladies.

A. DE TOCQUEVILLE.

Rome, April 22, 1851.

My dear M. de Tocqueville,—Our motions have been so uncertain that I could not venture to write before, but I now can tell you that we shall be in Paris either Friday the 2nd or Saturday the 3rd of May.

Ampère will tell you all our news up to about ten days ago. We have been most rigorous sight-seers, and are so sick of seeing that we have serious thoughts of shutting ourselves up and resolving not to see another sight for six months.

There is, however, not a sight but a *hearing* for which I am anxious, and that is your Assembly. I have very often been troublesome to you about it before and venture to be so again, and to beg you if you can get me a good card of admission to do so.

We are very happy to think that we shall so soon see you and Madame de Tocqueville again.

We look back to Sorrento as the pleasantest part of our tour.

Best regards to you both from us all.

Ever yours,
N. W. SENIOR.

CONVERSATIONS.

Paris, Rue de la Paix, May 3, 1851.—We left Italy on the 27th of April, and passed the 30th at Marseilles, with the Palmers, eminent machine makers. They complained bitterly of the commercial state of France. They merely execute orders : as the wants of the purchasers of machines are peculiar, each man requiring his own form, construction, and power, they cannot accumulate stock. Ever since 1841 those who ought, and used, to be their customers have been without confidence in the security of persons and property, and therefore have suspended as far as was possible all expensive operations. What is the real danger, they can seldom explain, but they keep repeating, 'Ça ne peut pas durer;' 'Quelque chose arrivera;' and these indistinct fears keep them inactive. Before 1848 they kept 1,000 workmen, now they engage only 400, and have the greatest difficulty in keeping these employed.

Rue de la Paix, May 4.—I went early in the morning to see Tocqueville, and found him sitting with Beaumont. I related my conversation with the Palmers at Marseilles.

'The Marseillais are quite right,' said Beaumont, ' in

believing that "ça ne peut pas durer;" but they are wrong in the importance they attach to a revolution. A revolution no longer interrupts the ordinary progress of society. The whole machinery of Government continues to work much in the same way, whatever be the changes in the moving power which directs it. Justice, police, revenue—in short, the whole interior administration for which Government is instituted, go on by force of the original impulse given to them under the Convention, and under the Empire; just as the human heart beats, and the human lungs play, independently of the will of their possessor. This is the most consoling result of our recent experience. If, as it seems probable, we are to pass the rest of our lives among revolutions, it is some comfort that a revolution is no longer the period of destruction, or even of disorganisation, that it once was.'

'The political horizon,' said Tocqueville, 'is darker, that is to say, obscurer, than I ever knew it to be. At Sorrento I thought that I could see a little before me. Since I am in Paris I give up all attempts at prophecy or even conjecture. One thing only is certain, that a legal solution of the questions that will have to be decided next year is impossible. The President will not consent to consider himself ineligible. Even if he were to do so, his friends would not act on that supposition. He will certainly be on the list of candidates, and the result perhaps most to be desired, or least to be deprecated, is that he should be re-elected by a majority so large as to be considered to speak the voice of the nation, and therefore to legalise its own act though opposed to the existing law. It must be remembered that by that time the new Assembly will have been elected, and the present Assembly therefore, though technically possessed of its full powers, will have lost its moral influence, and will be unable to oppose the public will.

'But even this result, though less formidable than the simultaneous change of the holders of all executive power and of all legislative power, will be an event of which the certain mischief will be great, the possible mischief enormous. What will be the effect on men's minds of a violation of the Constitution deliberately made by the nation, at the instigation of its chief magistrate? Who will respect a Constitution which the people has set aside in one of its most important provisions? That Constitution, bad as it is, is our only bulwark. Nothing else stands between us and either anarchy or despotism. The President is formidable enough as he is. What will he be when his mere election will have been a triumph over the only restraint that keeps him in—the Constitution? It is difficult even now to protect property from systematic plunder, and authority from organised revolt. What will be the difficulty after the Executive itself for many months has been employing thousands of agents to urge the people to break the law and has succeeded? Every exit seems besieged by some frightful spectre.

'At present there is a lull; parties are preparing for the discussion as to the revision of the Constitution, which cannot come on until the 28th.'

May 8.—Mrs. Grote and I drank tea with Tocqueville.

We talked of V.'s[1] theory as to the unfitness of France for a mixed Government.

'I do not see,' said Tocqueville, 'why what *has been*, should not be again. We endured a mixed Government for thirty-three years, why should we be incapable of enduring one now?

'I admit, however, that in order to enable a Government, in which the supreme power is divided, to be permanent; to last, as yours has done, for centuries, the ruling authorities must possess an amount of patience and forbearance which never has been granted to ours, and therefore I do not expect a mixed Government in France to be permanent, that is to say to be uninterrupted. Among thousands of possibilities, that which appears to me the least improbable is, that during the greater part of the next hundred years, France will be subject to a Constitutional Monarchy, from time to time interrupted by a despotic or by a democratic revolution.'

'Of course,' I said, 'the form of mixed Government under which you are living will not last?'

'Of course,' he answered, 'it will not. A despotic monarchy, or a despotic aristocracy, may retain its power for centuries, against the will of its subjects, but an unpopular democracy sounds like a contradiction in terms, and must soon become a contradiction in fact. As soon as the people has found the means of ascertaining and expressing its will, it will select, or accept, or

---

[1] For this conversation see Senior's *Journals in France.*—ED.

submit to the master whom it prefers to self-government.

'Those who imposed on us this Constitution knew that it would be unpopular; they tried to prolong its existence, first by pre-determining the mode in which it should be altered, and secondly by making that legal mode almost impracticable. Three quarters of the Assembly will not join in the vote, from which a third, perhaps nearly a half, of its members fear much more than they hope.'

'Will you then break,' I said, 'the band which you cannot untie—will you proceed to a revision on a simple majority?'

'I believe,' he answered, 'that the Government will make the attempt—and it was the fear of having to do this that prevented my friends and me from taking office. The danger of such a course is enormously increased by the new electoral law. Under a system of universal suffrage, the new Constituent Assembly could not have been said to be illegally elected. It would really have represented the whole nation. Now it will represent only a minority. Those who wish to resist its acts may proclaim them void, as the acts of a political body doubly illegal—illegally convoked and illegally nominated. The whole conduct and tone of the present administration convinces me that they have considered this risk and are resolved to encounter it. They are bolder than I am.'

Wednesday, May 14.—Before breakfast I sat for some

time with Tocqueville. We talked of the ministerial plans.

'To hope,' said Tocqueville, 'for a legal majority of the revision, is childish; though I have no doubt that an actual, and even a considerable one will be obtained. But I do not believe that that majority will sanction a revision in defiance of the law. Nor do I think that the Government will make the attempt without the sanction of the Assembly. It would be a "politique à se casser le cou, même à se faire couper le cou." If the President attempts it, he will find himself in Vincennes.'

'What then,' I asked, 'will the Government do?'

'Nothing,' he answered; 'it will drift down the current, and that current is carrying us towards a rock, towards a Rouge Assembly.

'I have always told you,' he continued, 'that there is no danger of a Rouge Assembly unless the Government create it. This Government *is* creating it. Its administration is a blister to the country. Everything is done that can irritate the friends of progress and even of liberty.

'Faucher[1] is a man of great honesty, great courage, and great knowledge—except the knowledge of men. He is active, obstinate, and injudicious. Such men are the ruin of a ministry, indeed of a party.'

'What are the faults,' I asked, 'to which you refer when you describe this as an irritating Government?'

'In this country,' he answered, 'the whole nature of

---

[1] M. Faucher was at this time Prime Minister.—ED.

the internal administration depends on the impulse and direction given to it by its chiefs.

'According to the instructions of the minister, any given law is executed loosely and indulgently, or strictly, or not at all. Under Faucher all is rigour and vigour. All the strings are stretched to the utmost. National guards are disbanded. Mayors are dismissed. Journals are suspended. The hand of Government is everywhere felt, and everywhere presses heavily.'

Saturday, May 17.—I found Tocqueville with us this afternoon when I returned from the Duc de Broglie's.

He asked me what were the Duc de Broglie's views,[1] and was glad to hear that he was determined to stand by the Republic.

'The Monarchical parties,' he said, 'are contemptible; the Legitimists are hated and feared by nine-tenths of the people; the Orleanists are a set of generals without an army; the Bonapartists have an army but no leaders.'

But he does not share the Duke's expectation that on the question of revision the minority will yield.

'It might yield,' he said, 'if the majority were compact and earnest; it might yield if the majority were cordially supported by the nation. But the nation is divided; it knows that the Constitution is faulty, but it is not sure that it will be exchanged for anything better. It would see with pleasure a few points selected for amendment, but it looks forward with terror to a new Constituent

---

[1] See Senior's *Journals in France*, vol. ii. p. 200.—ED.

Assembly which may avow principles which were with difficulty rejected in 1848; which may bring back *le droit au travail* and *le droit au secours*. The majority shares these fears, and though it will vote for the revision, because it would be unable to justify to its constituents a refusal to amend what it admits to be defective, a large portion of it will not be sorry that the legal majority is not obtained.'

'But why,' I said, 'not vote for a restricted revision, for the covering only of what experience has shown to be palpable blots?'

'Because,' he answered, 'even a respectable majority cannot be obtained for the purpose. The instant you come to details, each party looks to its own interests, and there is scarcely a point on which even three out of five agree. I own that I am inclined to think that one of the least objectionable parts of our Constitution is the difficulty which it throws in the way of change. The framers foresaw that the period of revision would be one of great danger, and they wisely endeavoured to postpone it, at least until the experiment of the Republic should have been made. This has not yet been done; for a Constitution which all who administer it are striving to overthrow, cannot be said to have been fairly tried. This general desire for revision is not the result of an appreciation of the merits and defects of the Constitution—it is the restlessness of a sick man who wishes to turn in his bed. All parties seem convinced that the revision will produce some form of Monarchy. Hence the violence with which it is urged on by the anti-Republicans and opposed by the Montagne. I do not share this conviction. Under our system of voting by lists, a compact minority which concentrates all its votes on its own candidates, has a great chance of beating a divided majority which supports as many candidates as it contains factions. I should not be surprised at seeing Rouge representatives from many of the departments on which the anti-Republican parties now rely. So clearly do I see the dangers of the revision, that I could not bring myself to vote for it, if I saw any other less dangerous course. But danger surrounds us on every side. Great and general as the alarm is, I believe it to be less than that which is justified by our situation.

'The Constitution,' he added, 'with all its defects might be endurable, if we could only believe in its permanence. But we read History. We see that republican institutions have never lasted in France, and we infer that those which we have now must be short-lived. This reading of History is our bane. If we could forget the past, we might apply a calm impartial judgment to the present. But we are always thinking of precedents. Sometimes we draw them from our own history, sometimes from yours. Sometimes we use the precedent as an example, sometimes as a warning. But as the circumstances under which we apply it always differ materially from those under which it originally took place, it almost always misleads us.

'We indicted Louis XVI. for conspiracy against the

nation, because you had indicted Charles I. We substituted Louis Philippe for Charles X. as you had substituted Mary for James.

'Louis XVI. believed that Charles I. had lost his crown and his life by raising his standard at Edge Hill. So he tried non-resistance. Charles X. saw that his brother's submission was fatal, and had recourse to the *ordonnances* and to his army. Louis Philippe recollected the fate of Charles X. and forbad his troops to act. Thus the pendulum oscillates, and generally oscillates wrong.'

Thursday, May 22.—Before breakfast I called on Tocqueville. We talked of the prospects of Louis Napoleon.

'They have become far less favourable,' said Tocqueville, 'during the last six months, and are darkening every day.

'There are three modes only in which he can attempt to retain power. One, of course, is through the revision of the Constitution; but this is not practicable, unless the state of public feeling not only changes, but runs in a direction opposite to its present current. The Chamber will not by the legal majority *vote* the revision, and will not, in the absence of that majority, sanction the revision.

'Another is a *coup d'état*. He may summon a Constituent body in defiance both of the Constitution and of the Assembly. This too would fail; the national guards and the army would side with the Assembly. It is very doubtful whether the Assembly and the

President together could effect a *coup d'état.* Neither of them could do so in opposition to the other.

'The last means is to be re-elected, though an illegal candidate, by an overwhelming majority. If this be his plan, his whole conduct is opposed to it. For that purpose he ought to be on good terms with the Assembly : he is constantly attacking it. He ought to appear to have no selfish views : all that he does seems to be prompted by personal motives—by vanity as respects the present, by ambition as respects the future. His administration ought to be as conciliatory as the safety of the country will allow it to be. Its roughness and insolence, its arbitrary dismissal of public functionaries, its suspension of newspapers, its interference in elections, the rudeness of its subordinates—in short, its generally irritating and unscrupulous character, are making enemies every day. In my own department, La Manche, one of the most conservative in France, the Rouge candidates, though happily still in a minority, are twice as strong as they were six months ago. Either he does not know what his ministers are doing, or he does not know what the effect of such a system must be.'

'Though the revision of the Constitution,' I said, 'is impossible at present, the time for it must come. Do you think that an Upper Chamber will be one of the elements of the new one ?'

'I hope,' he continued, 'that it will be. I voted for it and I shall vote for it again. A single Chamber seems to me to be a bad instrument of legislation. Still, however, as an antagonistic force, as a means of keeping in check the enormous power which we have given to our executive, it is more efficient than a double Chamber. I think that the Assembly has resisted the encroachments of the President better than could have been done by two Houses, each employing only a portion of the supreme legislative authority.'

'I suppose,' I said, 'that you will in time return to Hereditary Monarchy.'

'It would be rash,' he answered, 'to say that we shall not, but I do not see my way to it. The Fusion does not gain ground. In fact, what is called Fusion by the Orleanists is simply going over to the Legitimist side; for what do they get for the party which they call their own? They offer to make Henri V. King; and what is he to do for them in return? To acknowledge that the Comte de Paris is his cousin and heir—which will not be more certain, nor more notorious than it was before. The Anti-Fusionists of the Orleans party hate the Fusionists more bitterly even than they do the Legitimists.'

'What are Thiers' views?' I asked.

'His conduct,' answered Tocqueville, 'is inexplicable. He is attacking the President, the Republicans, and the Legitimists with a violence which, if his power were equal to his animosity, would end in bringing on some great catastrophe. His opposition to the Fusionists may perhaps be explained, for he sees Guizot among them, and you may often predict what will be the conduct of Thiers or of Guizot, if you know what the other will do. But knowing, as he must do, that the immediate restoration of the Orleanist branch is impossible, he must, one would think, know that his attacks on every other means of government must, if they could succeed, produce anarchy.'

May 23.—Z. paid me his promised visit.[1]

The Tocquevilles drank tea with us, the first time that either of them had ventured out in the evening.

I repeated my conversation with Z.

'I think,' said Tocqueville, 'that Z. is too confident as to the maintenance of the law of the 31st of May. It is impossible to deny that that law is inconsistent with a Constitution which professes to rest on universal suffrage. It is impossible to deny that in many places, especially in the country, it has worked exceedingly ill; that its obscurity has frequently occasioned it to be misinterpreted, and not seldom has enabled the persons entrusted with the register to admit or reject claims according to the politics of the claimant; and that it has disfranchised many hundreds of thousands on technical grounds. The pressure on the Assembly for its repeal will be great. The Montagne however, by its intemperance, is doing all it can to force the Assembly to retain its law as a point of honour. That party is probably not unwilling that so irritating a grievance should be kept alive. But the decision may not rest with the Assembly. It is true that if the President were to attempt a *coup d'état* for an obviously selfish purpose, he would fail. But I am not sure that he would fail if he were to try a popular

---

[1] See Senior's *Journals in France*, vol. ii. p. 216.

coup d'état. It is not easy to resist the combined action of the mob and the executive.

'The new electoral law is eminently unfavourable to the prolongation of his power; it disfranchises his supporters, and it will prevent his re-election from being the work of the nation. It is a favourite too with his enemy the Assembly. There are strong reasons for his striving to get rid of it by force; and he is quite rash enough to make the attempt.'

Tocqueville was amused by Z.'s enumeration of the concessions made by the Legitimists, and would not admit that the Orleanists gave up nothing.

'It is true,' he said, 'that they have no legal claims to the Crown. It is true that they have few friends; and it follows that they have no immediate chance of success. I foresee no possible combination of events which during the next three or four years would enable them to mount the throne to the exclusion of Henri V. But it is not true that they have no prospects, no *avenir*. If they have fewer friends than Henri V., they have fewer enemies. They offer to the French people a form of Government which suits us far better than a Republic, and they offer it untainted by the feudal insolence of the old *régime*, or by the wars and calamities of the Empire.

'The least objectionable Monarchy would be the Monarchy of the Comte de Paris. As I said before, that is now impossible. The Protestantism of the Duchess of Orleans is alone an insurmountable objection. It opposes to her the whole influence of the clergy, and that influence is stronger now than it has been since the death of Louis XIV.

'Nothing so much strengthened the Legitimists as the Protestantism which surrounded the Orleanists. But a few years hence, when the age of the Comte de Paris diminishes the fear of his mother's influence; when Guizot has retired from politics to history; when we are thoroughly tired of Presidents and Executive Commissions, we may think of using *la branche cadette*, as the best lever to raise us out of the mire of liberty, equality, and fraternity.

'In co-operating to bring back Henri V. the Orleanists give up this chance. It may not be great, but it is something.'

We left Paris on the next morning.

CORRESPONDENCE.

Versailles, July 2, 1851.

My dear Senior,—One of my best friends, who is at the same time a very distinguished member of our Assembly, M. de Combarel, is going to pass a few days in London with Madame de Combarel. I recommend them very particularly to your kindness, and shall be grateful for any attentions which you may be inclined to confer on them. M. de Combarel is well informed as to the complicated state of our affairs, and you will be glad to discuss them with him.

Living as I do in the country[1] and absorbed by the

[1] In July 1851 M. de Tocqueville inhabited a country-house near Versailles belonging to M. Rivet, and attended the Legislative Assembly. He

labour imposed on me by the commission for the revision, I was not able to visit Lord Monteagle till the day before he left Paris, when I did not find him at home. Pray be so good as to express to him my regret and make my excuses.

A. DE TOCQUEVILLE.

Kensington, July 15, 1851.

My dear Tocqueville,—The Combarels did not present themselves. They were probably too much engaged with the *matériel* of London to hunt up the *personnel*. I hope that we may be more fortunate another time.

was a member of a commission, in which MM. de Montalembert, Jules Favre, Berryer, De Corcelle, De Broglie, Charras, Cavaignac, Odillon Barrot, and Baze were among his colleagues, directed to consider the proposal for the revision of the Constitution. He was the *rapporteur*, and his report, dated the 8th of July, 1851 (No. 2064 of the papers of that year), is a masterly production, but too long to be introduced *in extenso*. I cannot, however, resist the temptation of extracting a passage describing the Constitution of 1848.

'A single Chamber, exclusively entitled to make laws: a single man exclusively entitled to preside over the application of all laws, and the direction of all public affairs, each of them elected directly by universal suffrage: the Assembly omnipotent within the limits of the Constitution: the President required, within those limits, to obey the Assembly; but wielding, from the nature of his election, a moral force which makes his submission uneasy, and must suggest to him resistance, and possessed of all the prerogatives which belong to the executive in a country in which the central administration, everywhere active and everywhere powerful, has been created by monarchs, and for the purposes of monarchy:—these two great powers, equal as to their origin, unequal as to their rights, condemned by law to coerce one another, invited by law to mutual suspicion, mutual jealousy, and mutual contest, yet forced to live in close embrace, in an eternal *tête-à-tête*, without a third power, or even an umpire, to mediate or to restrain them—these are not conditions under which a government can be regular or strong.'--ED.

Well, your report is out, and has enchanted everybody. It has also convinced everybody, except perhaps me. You remember that when we talked over the question of the prolongation you thought the re-election of Louis Napoleon, though an illegal candidate, by a large majority—a majority speaking the voice of the people, the least objectionable solution. Perhaps his *Dijon échappée*, or perhaps his *allocution* at Poictiers, have induced you to change your mind.

I see now that you are less favourable to the *scrutin de liste*. There are few subjects on which so much may be said on each side, as on the comparative advantages and disadvantages of separate and collective voting.

We have all been spinning round in the whirlpool of the London season; but by next week it will become calmer.

Our politics are all as flat as possible. Papal aggression, or at least the bill against it, has been found out to be a humbug. Since I have been here I have read the Papal bull and Cardinal Wiseman's pastoral. They are written on the model of Chinese state papers. Nothing but puerile flatulence. It must be degrading to humanity to be governed, and directed spiritually and temporarily, by people who can seriously publish such nonsense.

Gladstone is come back foaming against Naples. Lord Aberdeen has shown me a letter of his which treats the King of Naples, and generally the Italian Governments, much worse than even my journals do. I see that on Italian matters we are becoming Carbonari, and look rather with hope than fear to the probability of a French army crossing the Alps to drive out the King, Grand Dukes, and Pope.

Kindest regards from us all to you and Madame de Tocqueville. Let us hear when you can.

Ever yours,
N. W. SENIOR.

Versailles, July 27, 1851.

My dear Senior,—I am satisfied with the general effect which my report has produced in France, and delighted by its reception in England. I care almost as much about what is said of me on your side of the Channel as I do for what is said of me on ours. So many of my opinions and feelings are English, that England is to me almost a second country intellectually.

How comes it that my reasons in favour of the revision have not convinced you? What inconsistency is there between this report and my conversations with you at Sorrento?

I then thought the unconstitutional re-election of the President very probable. I think so still. Although Louis Napoleon has effectually alienated the higher classes, and almost all our eminent political men; although his popularity among the lower classes has much diminished, and is diminishing every day; notwithstanding all this, I confess that I still think his re-election nearly inevitable, partly in consequence of the want of any competitor, and partly in consequence of our general anxiety. I believe that the Bonapartist current, if it can be turned aside at all, can be turned aside only by meeting a revolutionary current, which will be still more dangerous ; and lastly, I believe that if he were to be illegally re-elected, any amount of attack on our liberties would become possible.

So convinced was I of this six months ago, that I remember telling you that I should probably retire from public life in order to have nothing to do with a government which may try to destroy, in law or in fact, all constitutional institutions, and perhaps, exhausted as we are, might for a time succeed.

The government which I should prefer, if I thought it possible, would be a republic ; but, believing its continuance impossible, I should see without regret Louis Napoleon become our permanent ruler, if I could believe that he would be supported by the higher classes, and would be able and desirous to rule constitutionally. But I told you then that I did not believe either of these things to be possible, and all that I see convinces me that I was right.

The President is as proof against all constitutional ideas as Charles X. was. He has his own idea of legitimacy, and he believes as firmly in the imperial constitution as Charles X. did in divine right. Then he separates himself more and more every day from almost all the men whose talents or experience fit them for public business, and is reduced to rely on the instincts and passions of the *peuple*[1] properly so called. His

---

[1] The lower classes.—ED.

re-election, therefore, especially if illegal, may have disastrous consequences. And yet it is inevitable, unless resisted by an appeal to revolutionary passions, which I do not wish to rouse in the nation.

What is the result of this, but a desire for a revision, which may either, by changing the nature and the origin of the executive, render his re-election impossible, or by rendering it legal, may render it less dangerous?

Many persons in France, and some even in England, have reproached me for having stuck so firmly to the Constitution, and for having led the Assembly to declare its adherence. I have been accused even of having foreseen an illegal re-election, and of having urged the Assembly to resist one. This is an error, as anyone who reads carefully my report will see.

I do not foretell, I did not wish to foretell, what the Assembly will do, or ought to do, on an unconstitutional re-election. It will depend on circumstances, particularly on the number of votes. There might be a manifestation of public opinion to which it might be prudent and patriotic to yield.

What I have said, and made the Assembly say, is, that during the interval which separates us from 1852, no illegality is to be permitted; that no party, not even the Government, is to be allowed to propose an illegal candidate; that we must act, and force everyone else to act, in such a manner as to leave the nation mistress of herself, able to consult her own interests, and to follow her own opinions.

I have said all this as forcibly as I could. First,

because I thought that to say so was useful to the country. Secondly, because I thought that it was right that I should say this.

A time may come when I myself may think that the people ought to be allowed to violate the Constitution. But I will let this be done by others. My hand shall never strike the flag of law.

Then this agitation for revision has two motives—one, a sincere wish for it, in order to improve the Constitution ; the other, an intrigue for the purpose of undermining and injuring the Constitution. The former is mine ; the latter I cannot join in.

In fact our situation is more complicated, more inextricable, and less intelligible, than it has ever been. We are in one of those strange and terrible positions in which nothing is impossible, and nothing can be foreseen. What is least improbable is the re-election of the President, and also the election of a new Assembly less favourable to him than is generally expected. If this be so, unless Louis Napoleon should take advantage of the first popular impulse which will enable him to rise to absolute power, he may find himself again opposed and hampered by a hostile Assembly.

The nation, though in this strange position, unexampled in history, is perfectly calm and not unprosperous. Trade, excepting agriculture, which has not recovered, does not fall off, perhaps increases. No one ventures on large speculations, but everyone eagerly and perseveringly follows his own business, as if all that is to happen to-morrow were not uncertain. Yet no one can see 1852 approach without terror—great, perhaps exaggerated. We have all, however, been educated by revolutions. We all know that it is our fate to live like a soldier in a campaign, whom the chance of being killed to-morrow does not prevent from caring for his dinner, his bed, and even his amusements. We are all in this position. When I see the attitude of the nation, I must admire it, and confess that, with all its follies and its weaknesses, it is a great people.

Your expectation that the habits of your people will render the Ecclesiastical Titles Act inoperative, seems to me probable. But why enact laws worse than your usages? I confess that I agree with all my heart and soul with those who, like Lord Aberdeen and Mr. Gladstone, oppose, in the spirit of liberty and of free institutions, those vain but dangerous attacks on liberty of conscience. Whither will religious freedom fly if she is driven from England? If those whose principle is freedom of inquiry and toleration become intolerant, what right have they to reproach the intolerance of Rome? Rome, if she violates the conscience of individuals, does not violate her own principles.

It is imprudent to criticise a foreign country, but I cannot but think that, a few years hence, the disturbance created by the Papal Aggression will be compared to the passions which two centuries ago produced the belief in the Popish Plot. This agitation is less violent, but no less unreasonable. Even those who now take part in it will be as little able to account for their conduct as we are.

Ever yours,
A. DE TOCQUEVILLE.

London, July 29, 1851.

My dear Tocqueville,—A thousand thanks for your valuable and interesting letter.

I think I must have ill explained myself in my last, for I do not think that you have perfectly understood me.

When we talked over the prospects of France last year and this year, you thought the legal revision almost impossible: you thought an illegal revision impossible. You thought it, however, probable that Louis Napoleon, though an illegal candidate, would be re-elected.

So far you have not changed your opinion. But it seems to me that you have changed it on another point.

You seemed to me then inclined to think that Louis Napoleon's illegal re-election, though a very dangerous event, would be less dangerous than any other solution of the present difficulties. And therefore you were, I think, favourable to its taking place.

Since that time the objections to his re-election seem to preponderate in your mind. His subsequent conduct may have strengthened the personal objections to him; or further reflection may have given additional force to the constitutional objections. This seems to me to be certain, that his chances of re-election are much diminished by your report. You have put forth, in language that never can be forgotten, arguments against it which cannot be refuted.

'If it had been possible,' you say, 'you would have preferred retaining the Republic.' I rather suppose that you prefer a republic, not to a constitutional monarchy, but to such a constitutional monarchy as, under the circumstances of the case, you are likely to have. The great misfortune of modern Europe seems to me to be the want of aristocracies; at least of good ones. Those of Belgium and Holland I believe are the best on the Continent, but though rich and well-disposed, they are not very intelligent. You might, I think, if you altered your law of succession, and allowed a man to dispose of his property as he liked, create one. For you are active and saving, and large fortunes would, I think, be permanent if once formed.

I quite agree in your vituperation of the Ecclesiastical Titles Bill. The Government fancy themselves forced to carry it, but they are very much ashamed of it; and I have no doubt that the Attornies-General for Ireland and for England, without whose consent no prosecution under it can take place, have had instructions to make it a dead letter.

Have you seen Gladstone's two letters to Lord Aberdeen on Naples? They are very striking. One of your countrymen informs me that he has ascertained that Lord Palmerston is furious at the superiority in our Exposition of the French products. That he is, therefore, preparing a new French revolution in order to crush your industry, and supplies the expense of a daily dinner of 200 conspirators!

Kindest regards to Madame de Tocqueville. Mrs. Senior is not yet quite recovered, but is going on well. We go to Great Malvern, Worcestershire, on the 7th.

Ever yours,
N. W. SENIOR.

Kensington, November 30, 1851.

My dear Tocqueville,—I sent to you by Mrs. Grote the Sorrento and Paris journals, those in which you are most interested, for they derive their whole value from your conversation. I have had your last letter copied at the end of the Paris journal, but on trying to correct it I found the copy so hopelessly corrupt that I gave it up. I wish that you could find time to look at it and correct it. Any remarks on the journals will of course be very valuable. If you think fit to show both or either of them to Beaumont, I can have no objection.

We are all looking anxiously across the Channel. Your conversations have so much prepared me for the events which have passed since May, that I seem to be looking at a play which I have read in manuscript.

You would not, however, reveal the *dénouement*, but your fears as to the result of an alliance between the President and the mob have often occurred to me.

Palmerston is rising with us. We think that he has done nothing very monstrous for some time, unless the sending Gladstone's pamphlet about be so considered.

Kindest regards from us all to you and Madame de Tocqueville.

Ever yours,
N. W. SENIOR.

To N. W. Senior, Esq.

Paris, November 28, 1851.

I was beginning, dear friend, to complain of your silence when your letter reached me. I read it with great pleasure, and it gave me still more pleasure to talk of you with our friend, Mrs. Grote, who is as agreeable as ever, but who seems to me to be less well in health than the last time that she was in Paris.

I had already heard, and Mrs. Grote, whom I questioned on the subject, confirmed to me, that you had been offered a high place in India.[1] It was not right in you to tell me nothing about it, as you know the deep interest which I take in all that concerns you. It seems, however, that there was not much in it. I am delighted. I own that I should like you to leave England, but not to go so far, or to such a completely different climate. It would not have suited your friends, nor, perhaps, your health. What I should wish for you would be some important post in the Mediterranean, which would insure your keeping well, and enable such of your friends as, like myself, find great enjoyment in your society, to obtain it from time to time.

[1] Mr. Senior had been offered the post of Legislative Member of Council at Calcutta.—ED.

Permit me not to allude to our public affairs, in spite of the gravity of the present circumstances, or rather, on account of that very gravity. Not that there is any obstacle to the freest discussion. But our thoughts are so painful that the best way is not to express them, and even to try, if possible, not to think. There are things which cannot be contemplated calmly when they are close at hand, even though they may have been long foreseen. Our present condition is one of these things. It can end only by some great catastrophe. My clear view of the magnitude and of the proximity of the calamity is so bitterly painful that I try as much as possible to divert from it my thoughts.

Mrs. Grote has forwarded to me the two valuable volumes containing your recollections of Paris and Sorrento. Our state of perpetual though useless excitement has prevented my looking into them. But I fully intend to do so. I shall especially enjoy reading all that will recall to me Sorrento, and the busy yet peaceful months which I spent on the shores of the Bay of Naples. I often look back with tender regret to the place itself, and to the time that I spent there. That delicious and tranquil retreat, coming as it did between the revolution of 1848 and the one which is impending, was like a rest upon some Southern isle between two shipwrecks. Write to me sometimes if only to tell me how you are.

&c. &c. &c.
ALEXIS DE TOCQUEVILLE.

Kensington, November 30, 1851.

My dear Tocqueville,—I wrote nothing to you about the Indian matter, because I never thought very seriously about it. If my health were to fail, or if Masters in Chancery were abolished, I would accept it for a couple of years; but I hope that the former alternative will not take place, and I fear that the latter will not. So that I would bet 100 to 1 against my going to India.

I do not wonder at the grief with which you look at the present state of affairs in France. It fills me also with alarm and regret. I am very anxious to see the state of affairs a little nearer; and if Mrs. Grote stays till the middle of January, I think that I shall brave the cold, and be in Paris about the 2nd—I say the 2nd because I cannot venture to be there *le jour de l'an*.

To have to visit all one's friends in one day of about four hours, and carry about with one a hundred packets of useless trifles to be distributed with pretty speeches, would be worse than a Carnival or a holy week in Rome.

I hear, without believing it, that you are thinking of again quitting Paris for a time. If, however, there should be any truth in the report, I trust that we may hope for you here. Your and Madame de Tocqueville's apartments stand vacant for you, and our winter, bad as it is, is not so bad as yours.

On Friday, an agreeable American, a Mr. Walker, came to us. I mention him to you because I believe that he intends to call on you. He was Polk's Secretary of the Treasury.

Kindest regards from us all to you and to Madame de Tocqueville.

Ever yours truly,
N. W. SENIOR.

END OF THE FIRST VOLUME.

LONDON: PRINTED BY
SPOTTISWOODE AND CO., NEW-STREET SQUARE
AND PARLIAMENT STREET

www.ingramcontent.com/pod-product-compliance
Lightning Source LLC
Chambersburg PA
CBHW032058220426
43664CB00008B/1057